The
SWAN
CURRICULUM

The SWAN
CURRICULUM

Create a Spectacular New You with
12 Life-Changing Steps in 12 Amazing Weeks

Nely Galán

WITH BRONWYN GARRITY

10 ReganBooks
Celebrating Ten Bestselling Years
An Imprint of HarperCollins*Publishers*

All photographs courtesy of Fox.

This book contains advice and information relating to health care. It is not intended to replace medical advice and should be used to supplement rather than replace regular care by your doctor. It is recommended that you seek your physician's advice before embarking on any medical program or treatment. All efforts have been made to assure the accuracy of the information contained in this book as of the date of publication. The publisher and the author disclaim liability for any medical outcomes that may occur as a result of applying the methods suggested in this book.

HarperCollins books may be purchased for educational, business, or sales promotional use. For information please write: Special Markets Department, HarperCollins Publishers Inc., 10 East 53rd Street, New York, NY 10022.

FIRST EDITION

Designed by Kris Tobiassen

Printed on acid-free paper

Library of Congress Cataloging-in-Publication Data

Galán, Nely, 1963–
    The swan curriculum : create a spectacular new you with 12 life-changing steps in 12 amazing weeks / Nely Galán with Bronwyn Garrity. — 1st ed.
       p. cm.
    ISBN 0-06-076336-1
    1. Women—Psychology. 2. Women—Life skills guides.   I. Garrity, Bronwyn.   II. Title.

HQ1206.G35 2004
646.7'0082—dc22

                                                                                                2004051057

04 05 06 07 08 RRD 10 9 8 7 6 5 4 3 2 1

To Mike Darnell,
for making *The Swan* a reality,
with all of his passion, dedication, and creative brilliance.

To Nelida and Arsenio, my parents,
for trying to understand an unconventional daughter.

To Lukas, my son,
who finally brought clarity to my life
and taught me what is truly meaningful.

Acknowledgments

To Judith Regan, who has always believed in me and supported me, and Bronwyn Garrity, for "getting" my voice and working with inordinate speed. I am in awe of you. To Pablo Fenjves for his faith, humor, and for introducing me to Bronwyn. To Jessica Colter for encouraging us to do the impossible in record time. To the Swans who worked so hard to make their dreams come true and who made this book possible.

To Gail Berman, Sabrina Ishak, Tom Sheets, Wenda Fong, Stephanie VanHoff, and Meghan O'Sullivan for their creativity; Joe Early, Michael Roach, Kevin Spicer, Marisa Fermin, Donna Redier Linsk, Melissa Gold, and the rest of the gang at Fox; and to Carolyn Darnell whose support was unwavering.

To Arthur Smith and Kent Weed for executing my original idea so brilliantly; Jen Bresnan for the "no mirrors," Sean Atkins, Faye Stapleton, Carl Buehl, and the rest of the production staff for their time and commitment.

To Cecile Frot-Coutaz, David Shall, Jill Schwartz, Mike Jaffa, and the rest of the gang at Fremantle, my partners on the show, and to David Lyle who got me there.

To Mark Itkin, John Ferreter, Sam Haskell, Angela Petillo, Suzy Unger, Laurie Pozmentier, and the rest of the William Morris team for their faith.

To Susan Habif, my therapist, who in my darkest hour helped me find my way, and to my "group" (you know who you are). To Chevy Hernandez and Norma Carballo for being my backbone at GALAN Entertainment. To Kathleen Bedoya and Diana Mogollon, who always encouraged me to tell my stories and share my vulnerabilities. And to Manny Rodriguez, for his patience, love and support. Thanks, Pooh!

To the teachers and coaches who gave me tools—Sandra Cisneros, Pema Chodron, Reverend Michael Beckwith, Julia Cameron, Tony Robbins, and Al Reis. To all those who inspire me to do my work, which always takes me to a higher place.

He had been persecuted and despised for his ugliness, and now he heard them say he was the most beautiful of all the birds. Even the elder-tree bent down its bows into the water before him, and the sun shone warm and bright. Then he rustled his feathers, curved his slender neck, and cried joyfully, from the depths of his heart, "I never dreamed of such happiness as this, while I was an ugly duckling."

—HANS CHRISTIAN ANDERSEN,
THE UGLY DUCKLING

Contents

Preface

"Life isn't about finding yourself. Life is about creating yourself."

—GEORGE BERNARD SHAW

The way I see it, life is about both.

Take the story of *The Ugly Duckling*. A homely bird is chased from his home, attacked, cursed, and rendered too neurotic to live until he throws himself at the feet of some passing swans screaming, "Kill me!" only to discover he has grown into a handsome swan himself.

I am the original Swan. About five years ago, I got stuck. By this I mean I crashed, burned, and got lost in the maze of life. Somewhere along the way, I had derailed from my goals and my values. Yes, I'm a television producer with my own company. I have wonderful friends. I make good money. Unfortunately, none of this mattered when I discovered I was pregnant at the age of thirty-five. My boyfriend of eight years was the ultimate fixer-upper and I had no intention of marrying him.

At the same moment that I realized I had to have this baby, I knew I had to let my boyfriend go and raise my child as a single mother. It was the most excruciating and confusing period of my life. It seemed absurd. I was a career girl. I didn't know the first thing about single motherhood. You see, I'm from a Catholic Latino background where such things happen . . . to other girls. And I'd spent my life distinguishing myself from these other girls. From a young age, I made my career a priority, and it had paid off. I was sitting in business meetings with moguls. I created my own shows and television channels for a living. I always got exactly what

I wanted, and yet here I was, in the playground, with a congregation of single Latinas, watching my child brave the slide.

How could I, a woman who seemed to do everything right, be raising a baby alone? *I am having an out-of-body experience,* I told myself. *This isn't me.* But it was me. And I knew that if I did not thrive in this situation, I would perish.

As a television producer, I am trained to research anything. So, I performed research on my most important topic: *me.* I located the best self-help experts in the world. I attended therapy and Buddhist silent meditation retreats. I went back to church. I met with Tony Robbins and took his seminars. I read book after book after book to learn how to find focus, flow, and fun in life.

I should tell you that I'm not someone who believes in gurus; I don't accept anything at face value. I'm not what you would call "new-agey." My studies paid off because I hand-picked the lessons that resonated with me. Reinterpreting the teachings for myself, I wrote hundreds of pages in my diary. In time, these writings developed into simple exercises and graphs, which I completed monthly to chart my growth and help me repair the areas in my life that were not working.

Before long, other career girls who were experiencing various types of roadblocks were calling me to ask about the workbook. I found myself giving it to stay-at-home moms, professionals, students, and any other women I came across who were looking to evolve. (Even men were asking for it!) Those who used the book claimed that it helped them switch careers, change their appearance, and find love, wealth, and self-confidence. As I heard of more and more success stories, I realized I needed to work in this area, that I needed to share my method—I like to call it Swanning—with as many people as possible. That's how I came up with the idea for the television show, *The Swan.*

The Swan Curriculum is a refined version of my original workbook. If you commit to the process, your perspective on your life will shift. Change, I learned from the exercises that follow, is about perspective, about seeing possibilities where you once saw roadblocks. When I confront something negative these days, the first thing I tell myself is that it can be fixed. The key is to turn negatives into positives. If I hadn't broken up with the father of my son, if I hadn't had doubts about motherhood, if I hadn't suffered a work-related breakdown—in short, if my life had been easy and free of angst—I would *not* have my son, who is without a doubt the best thing that ever happened to me. I would *not* have the show or this book. I would *not* have been pushed to take my company to a whole new level, where I have the freedom to do only those things that touch my soul. I would *not* be as in love with my life as I am every day.

A few years ago, I reread Hans Christian Andersen's *Ugly Duckling* story with my son. I was amazed at how well it captured this experience of being flawed in a world obsessed with perfection. Of course, we women don't just wake up one day to find that we have become what we always dreamed; like the ugly duckling, we sometimes need assistance. That is why I created the television show *The Swan*—to help other women who are stuck. The show follows eighteen "ugly ducklings" throughout their four month commitment to self-transformation. During this time, they receive therapy, life coaching, fitness training, diet counseling and, yes, plastic surgery. Their transformations are amazing, but don't think what you're about to embark on is any less powerful. You have in front of you the very workbook I developed for my own transformation—into the original Swan.

Becoming a Swan requires faith. And I don't mean religion. I mean the faith that you'll be taken care of in the universe if you do your work.

Welcome to *The Swan Curriculum.*

NELY GALÁN
June 2004
Los Angeles, California

Introduction

Using This Book to Make Real Changes in Your Life

I can't speak for the male ducklings out there, but if you're female, I assure you, the day will come when you look at your life and think, "This sucks. I'm stuck." It doesn't matter if you're a Hollywood star or the checkout girl at Kmart. Whether it happens at twenty or thirty or forty-five I cannot tell you. But I do know it will happen.

Perhaps you are already aware of some stickiness in your life. Maybe your dream is to write a book, but you are so filled with self-doubt that you cannot complete a single chapter. Maybe marriage and children are your goals, but the only men you meet are jerks. Maybe you feel insecure about your looks. Maybe you have no idea why you wake up in the morning feeling listless and lost.

The truth is, of course, that your whole life doesn't suck; probably only a few things are out of place. We women tend to focus on the negative, and for good reason: Negative energy is potent. Unchecked, it can snowball into other areas of your life, affecting your self-esteem, your outlook, your productivity, even your health. But, if you use it to guide you, you

> "There are very few human beings who receive the truth, complete and staggering, by instant illumination. Most of them acquire it fragment by fragment, on a small scale, by successive developments, cellularly, like a laborious mosaic."
>
> —ANAÏS NIN

will reverse its charge, allowing it to spur you toward real, lasting change. You see, if you look at it from a different angle, getting stuck is the equivalent of receiving a wakeup call from the universe. Harness its power and you have found your secret weapon.

The Promise of The Swan

It is important that you embark on this project—self-transformation—with the determination, focus, and energy you would afford any other job. If you don't, you will stifle your own development.

The following "Swan Promises" will help you remember that your transition is an incredibly important and worthwhile full-time job. Read them carefully and sign each one—it is the first step in becoming a Swan!

SWAN PROMISE #1: I WILL NOT GIVE UP.

Commit to the twelve-week plan.

To become the Swan of your dreams, you will need to invest three months into your development. This may seem like a great deal of time, but compare it to what you would commit to a new job. Would you give a new position only two weeks to pan out before quitting? No. You'd work at it for three months, six months, or a year. As a Swan in training, you deserve the same effort.

Read and focus on one chapter each week, completing all of the exercises and spending ample time simply *contemplating*. As you move forward, keep in mind that these steps are designed for a *lifetime* of development. Yes, you will accomplish a great deal in three months. Yes, you will have achieved real change you can be proud of. But, your work represents a *beginning*. When you have finished the curriculum, you will have a roadmap toward your transformation. You will have a clearer idea about your goals and the obstacles you face. You will understand what you need to do to maintain the changes you have already affected. But, being the best person you can be is an ongoing process. It requires returning to these questions again and again, revisiting the "nest" whenever you need the help.

Accept fear as a part of the process.

Fear is an inevitable component of change. Who hasn't resigned herself to a boring job or toxic relationship because the alternative looked too much like a jump into the abyss? The unknown is terrifying, but terror can be a highly effective motivator. As a Swan, you will convert obstacles into the energy you need to propel yourself to the next phase. In order to make real, lasting change you must be willing to take risks and hold your course, even under the most daunting circumstances.

I understand that I may experience fear, restlessness, and an urge to close this book and go back to my old life. I promise to hold my course, complete the exercises, and stick to my routine for the duration of the three months I need to become a Swan.

_____

Signature

Stay Strong!

The Swan Cristina underwent quite a struggle after her painful surgery and repeatedly said she wanted to go home. She missed her family terribly and worried that she had made a mistake. But despite her pain, Cristina held her course and look at her now! She wound up as a contender in *The Swan* beauty pageant.

SWAN PROMISE #2: I WILL STICK TO MY ROUTINE.

Turn the new you into the everyday you.

When I first met the Swan Marnie she was depressed and hadn't dated for ten years. Although she stated her objectives as *finding a good relationship* and *rejuvenating herself* through plastic surgery and physical training, at first she didn't act on these goals with integrity. She didn't wear her chin-strap, essential after her plastic surgery. She fell asleep at the gym. She refused to leave her room for days at a time. Marnie was avoiding her routine and thus not opening herself up to the possibility of transformation. She was not allowing her goals to be real possibilities. How would she meet anyone if she stayed in her room? We sat down a number of times, and I dished out some tough love until Marnie began to adhere to her daily practice, ultimately transforming into one of the most beautiful Swans on the show.

The Swan Curriculum is a twelve-step program for women seeking change. Following this routine is the way to make the new you as much a part of your everyday as brushing your teeth. Once you have isolated your problem areas, you will devise a routine to guide and protect you as you begin to make changes. Your routine requires fastidious adherence for a few reasons:

"If you want something bad enough, the whole earth conspires to help you get it."

—MADONNA

- Each day you follow it will move you a step closer toward your ultimate goal.

- Regular practice will protect you from becoming either very depressed or overly happy. (It may sound strange, but both are destructive forces.) It means you will be more even keeled, and that you will be able believe in your new sense of self no matter what happens in your life.

- It will help you stay down to earth and remain the new you under any circumstances.

I will not stray from my routine. I will remind myself that I have signed this contract, a promise to see the process through one day at a time.

_____
Signature

SWAN PROMISE #3: I WILL LEARN TO EMBRACE CHANGE.

Be open to new ideas.

As a Swan, you will review your value system, your priorities, and the foundations on which you have built your life. For example, you may have always believed that plastic surgery was an exercise in superficiality, although you have often complained about the bags under your eyes. Looking closely at your beliefs will enable you to reaffirm the ones that work and alter those that are causing you difficulty. Having a clear understanding of your innermost convictions is necessary to turn your life around.

Fess up to your own weaknesses.

To make a change, you must be able to admit that there is a part of your life you cannot master. For me, having a satisfying and successful career is easy as pie. But ask me to cook dinner for twenty-five people and I will break out in hives. Similarly, if you ask me for dating tips, I will revert to a fifteen-year-old wallflower. We all have weak spots in our lives. If you want to overcome them, you need to be honest about yours.

I will be open to new ideas, possibilities, and realities even when I would rather not face them.

_____
Signature

SWAN PROMISE #4: I WILL SEEK OUT EXPERTS.

Speak up when you need assistance.

For some reason, women are not willing to spend the same time, energy, and money on themselves as they do on their jobs and families. Routinely, I meet women who work twelve-hour days and say they can't find the time for a massage. One Swan, for example, was willing to spend any amount of money on her husband's every whim, but lived three decades with a nose that made her feel depressed and unattractive.

When I was twenty-three, I was hired to run a television station. The first day on the job I received some very complex financials with no instructions on what to make of them. I was in over my head.

So I thought, *Okay, I don't know anything about finance. Am I going to fake it? If I do, then I'll wake up one day and realize how little I've actually learned.* That wouldn't do. I tried to imagine what a really sensible person would do: She'd hire a math tutor. I hired a tutor to come to my office three times a week and teach me the tools of the trade. (I told everybody she was my consultant, and she *was.*) To this day, I can read financials with the best of them. And to whom do I owe that talent? To myself, for being honest about my shortcomings.

Avoid the competency trap.

No one is born into the world knowing everything he or she needs to know. While the foolish fake comprehension and avoid asking for help, a Swan knows when she needs assistance. Thankfully, experts exist in every field—from math to fitness to makeup application—to help you along your way. Invest in them—it doesn't have to be expensive. In fact, it might even be free if you use a little creativity and some persistence. A few years ago, for example, I read a guide for businesses looking for better focus. I was inspired and filled with questions and ideas I wanted to discuss with the author, Al Reis. I did some research and discovered that the author was very much in demand as a consultant to Fortune 500 companies. His fee? A staggering $50,000 per day—far beyond my means. *Oh well,* I thought, *I'll just leave a message or two or three and see if he calls me back.* One day he did just that, explaining that he wanted to donate his services to me for one day because he was impressed by my perseverance. I received a $50,000 discount because I asked for it.

If you ask for help, you just might receive it.

Do your homework.

Determining who can best assist in resolving your trouble areas will require research. Turn the Internet, the phonebook, and the grapevine into your best friends. Let's say you have identified

Invest in Yourself?

When I was made president of Telemundo (the second largest Spanish language television network in the country), I was concerned—not about the work, the stress, or the fact that I had to manage so many people—but about my lack of style. In those days, you see, I used to wear really tchotchke things, and people sometimes got the wrong idea about me. Who could help me? Why not a *Vogue* fashion editor? Surely she would have some great ideas for me. I didn't know if an editor would do such a thing, but I thought there was no harm in asking.

Indeed, the editor constructed a book for me in which she pasted snapshots of outfits and accessories for every day of the week. Suddenly, a burden was lifted from my shoulders. I learned the art of dressing and followed my little guidebook until I no longer needed it. Most importantly, I no longer had to worry about whether I was dressed appropriately. I knew I looked great. Now I was free to focus entirely on my job. And it was cheaper to hire her than to get my clothes from a store—she got me my entire wardrobe at wholesale prices!

Most department stores now have a personal shopping department where a professional shopper can help you improve your wardrobe for free as long as you buy the clothes there. Check it out.

your sense of style as a weak spot, and you are working to improve your personal presentation at work. Try sending out an e-mail to all of your friends, and let them know you are looking for a stylist to help out on a "project." Keep in mind that *no one* needs to know what your project is, not even the stylist. If you want to hire someone, try the website Craig's List (www.craigslist.org), or explore the infinite resources of the World Wide Web. Don't know how to use a computer? No problem. Go to your local library—the staff will be glad to help you for free. The point is, be a problem solver. All the resources in the world are right in front of you. To find them, just open your eyes.

I am willing to acknowledge when I need assistance and will not hesitate to seek it out.

_____

Signature

SWAN RULE #5: I WILL LET MYSELF BE A LITTLE BIT SELFISH.

Selflessness is a female virtue, isn't it?

No. Yet, we embrace the notion that a woman who gives totally of herself, without concern for her own well-being and fulfillment, is somehow nobler than the woman who gives something to others and saves at least as much for herself.

I find it horribly counterproductive that, as a society, we celebrate this impossible model of femininity. Everyday life is incredibly complicated and demanding. It isn't enough to be a loving wife and mother. The world also expects us to be sexy lovers and savvy businesswomen, and to be thin, beautiful, and seductive at the same time. We can meet all those expectations, certainly, if that's what we want. And most of the women I know *do* want that. And why not? We see perfect women everywhere—on television, in magazines and movies, on billboards!

I'm not perfect. None of us are. Even movie stars aren't born perfect. They make themselves that way. Sure, they have great genes to start with, but they also have trainers, plastic surgeons, housekeepers, nannies, therapists, and stylists. They have experts help them.

Why shouldn't you?

Choose the response(s) closest to the one just uttered by the nasty little critic in your head:

☐ 1. I'm not a movie star; it's not my job to look good.
☐ 2. I don't have the money for stuff like that.
☐ 3. I don't care that much about my looks.
☐ 4. I don't deserve it.
☐ 5. I can do it all myself.

(Most women utter some combination of all of the above.)

Selfishness and the Renaissance woman

Now, rather than attempting to change the world's (and your own) expectations of women, you need to find a way to work with what you have and achieve what is possible. Think of yourself as a Renaissance woman, embarking on a voyage of self-discovery, self-improvement, and self-empowerment. But to do this takes selfishness—time devoted nowhere but inward. And don't be shy about the *s* word. Selfishness is not a bad word. If you can't work on yourself, what good will you be to others? What good will you be as a lesser, diminished version of yourself? You owe it

> "Far better it is to dare mighty things, to win glorious triumphs, even though checkered by failure, than to take rank with those poor spirits who neither enjoy much, nor suffer much, because they live in the gray twilight that knows not victory nor defeat."
>
> —THEODORE ROOSEVELT

to yourself and those around you to be the you that you know in your heart you can be. The you that you *deserve* to be.

When you commit to the Swan Curriculum, you will be putting yourself first for the next three months. This does not mean you should leave your children, ignore your husband, and dispense with your friends and relatives, but you might let them know that you're busy with a project, and that you may not be available to everyone around the clock. On the other hand, if you use your time wisely, people might not even notice that you're off on the first phase of the adventure of a lifetime. Because, the truth is, all you really need is one hour a day—one entire, uninterrupted hour—when you can work on yourself, where you can begin to nourish the Swan that's hidden deep inside you.

There's one in all of us.

The One-Hour Appointment

For the television show, Swans are sequestered in an apartment complex where they work on themselves day in and day out with therapists, life coaches, trainers, nutritionists, and surgeons. You will get many of the same benefits without the isolation simply by scheduling time alone for yourself.

Swan Assignment: To begin on your path toward a little bit of much-needed selfishness, schedule a one-hour appointment with yourself every day this week. Write it in your calendar; make it formal. If your day is impossibly packed, set the alarm one hour early and sit in the kitchen with a cup of coffee and your workbook. Better yet, take a morning walk to the park and do your work in the sunshine.

I agree to find time for myself every day for the duration of my course along The Swan Curriculum.

_____
Signature

"I learned that courage was not the absence of fear, but the triumph over it. The brave man is not he who does not feel afraid, but he who conquers that fear."

—NELSON MANDELA

SWAN PROMISE #6: I WILL LEARN TO APPRECIATE MYSELF.

Don't wait ten years too long.

When I look at pictures of myself from ten years ago, it makes me sad to know that I thought I was ugly back then. I wasn't ugly. I just didn't know how to appreciate myself. It's tragic how many other women out there are also unable to enjoy their lives because of their insecurities. That's how I came up with the idea for *The Swan*. I wanted to help women appreciate themselves, to make the changes and do the work to make themselves better instead of spending all their time wishing they were someone else.

Here's to appreciating your own wonderful life!

I promise to make every effort to appreciate myself and my life, and to refrain from making negative comments about myself.

_____

Signature

The Swan Contract

It's time to make it official!

When you're ready to begin the program, sign this final contract with yourself.

I promise to allow myself the time and attention necessary to make real changes happen in my life. I understand that certain exercises may be uncomfortable and challenging, but I will resign myself to the process because I deserve to be the best woman I can be.

_____

Signature

YOUR NEW MANTRA

For three months, you will place yourself at the center of your universe and finally realize that you are the most important project in your life. At the start of your first day, week, or month in the program, read the Swan Mantra aloud:

I deserve to be the best woman I can be.
I deserve to take time for myself every day.
I deserve to make changes to my life and my body as I see fit.
I deserve to be beautiful.
I deserve to be happy.
I deserve passion.
I deserve love.
I deserve to be fit.
I deserve to be indulgent sometimes.
I deserve the same time and energy that I afford my job, my husband, and/or my family.

Congratulations, and welcome to the beginning of the rest of your life!

Swan Secret: Commitment is the first step toward success.

The Areas of Your Life

The Path to a Positive Perspective

"My whole life sucks."

I hear this statement with alarming frequency from Swans. Yet, oddly, when I ask *why*, few people have a better answer than "It just does." Still, I know the feeling. You wake up feeling as down as a slug in the sun, only to discover new woes as the day wears on. You have a touch of adult acne, say, or your pointy ears look even pointier today. A new wrinkle just cropped up. Suddenly, you're cursing the day you were born.

It doesn't matter how long a list of grievances you can reel off. Your whole life does not suck. What sucks is feeling crappy. The remedy? A little perspective, some acknowledgment of life's many components, and an appreciation for what is going *right*.

There was a time when I focused only on the negatives in my life. My diaries are filled with poignant questions, such as, "Why don't I have a husband?" and "Why doesn't my body look the way I want it to?" For some reason, I never asked, "Why are my parents healthy?" or "Why do I have magical friends and a great brain that allows me to focus on anything and make it happen?"

When I look back through my diaries, it's disappointing to find no record of the joys or successes. In these older diaries, I have no record of what was working, no understanding of why something succeeded, and thus no path to lead me there again.

Time to Take Stock

Human beings have a penchant for the negative. For whatever reason, our instinct is to focus on the one thing that is wrong instead of the ten things that are right. Acknowledging the positive is critically important to your transformation. I devised the *Areas of Your Life* to help you regain perspective and to see that, yes, maybe a few things suck today, but there are several more that are won-

> "A person who aims at nothing is sure to hit it."
>
> —ANONYMOUS

derful. This section can help you take the self-doubt and disappointment you sometimes wake up to and break it down into visible, manageable components.

Use the worksheet below to take a stock of your life, piece by piece. What comes easily to you? What has always been a challenge? Where do you want to make changes? Allow yourself to free associate—to consider and jot down anything that pops into your head.

☐ **WORK** What do you do to make money?

_____

_____

☐ **VOCATION** What is the key to your true happiness?

_____

_____

☐ **LOVE** Who loves and cares for you?

_____

_____

☐ **EDUCATION** What are you learning in the world?

_____

_____

☐ **FAMILY & FRIENDS** Are the people around you truly supportive?

_____

_____

☐ **FORGIVENESS** Do you hold on to the things that have hurt you?

_____

_____

☐ **SPIRITUALITY** Where do you find faith?

_____

_____

☐ **FUN** What gives you joy?

_____

_____

☐ **COMMUNITY** How do you acknowledge and express your gratitude?

_____

_____

☐ **SEX** Is your intimate life bringing you vitality?

_____

_____

☐ **HEALTH & FITNESS** What do you do to care for yourself?

_____

_____

☐ **BEAUTY** What do you do to maintain your appearance?

_____

_____

_____

The Areas Exercise

1. Review the worksheet and make a small check in each box representing a part of your life you feel is *not* a problem area.

2. List the number of checked boxes: _____

3. Draw a small circle around each box representing a part of your life you feel *is* a problem area.

4. List the number of circled boxes: _____

5. Most likely, the circled problem areas are the parts of your life you think suck. If suck equals circle, how many parts of your life suck? _____

    List the circled categories. (Notice that there are only eleven spaces. I'm not allowing you the option that everything is a problem.)

i. _____	vi. _____
ii. _____	vii. _____
iii. _____	viii. _____
iv. _____	ix. _____
v. _____	x. _____
	xi. _____

6. Jot down some notes in each checked category about what is working. Just a few words are necessary, but if you like, use a separate sheet of paper to elaborate, and staple or paper clip it to this page after we move on.

7. *Free Association Excavation:* For each circled box, write down whatever comes to mind. This is an exercise in free association, meaning you can use this space to discuss anything important to you about this topic. For example, if you feel that work is an area in your life that could use some help, you might discuss issues you encounter in your current job or past jobs, or write about your ideal job. In other words, write whatever comes to mind, with as much detail as you care to include. If you need more room, include separate sheets of paper and staple them into your book for later reference.

Additional notes:

_____

_____

_____

_____

_____

_____

_____

_____

_____

_____

_____

_____

_____

_____

_____

_____

_____

_____

_____

_____

_____

_____

"Determine what specific goal you want to achieve. Then dedicate yourself to its attainment with unswerving singleness of purpose, the trenchant zeal of a crusader."

—PAUL J. MEYER, MOTIVATIONAL THERAPIST

If We Focus, We Accomplish

Every time you do the *Areas* section you'll find at least one part of your life in need of attention. But keep in mind no one on the planet has a life free from imperfections. Most people I work with circle at least two or three areas, but many others isolate *several* more. But several is not a whole life; it's a piece of a life, a *manageable* fraction. By pointing out these trouble areas, you make it easier to focus and say, "Okay, this is not so bad. I can do this."

ASKING THE RIGHT QUESTIONS

When we're down in the dumps, we ask stupid questions, such as "Why me?" In turn, our brains give us stupid answers: "Because you're a loser." If you ask yourself the *right* questions, you'll be amazed by the specific answers you get. As you work your way through this book, consider the way in which you question yourself. For example, *why* never gave anyone a satisfying answer, whereas *what* yields specifics you can use.

> "Most people have no idea of the giant capacity we can immediately command when we focus all of our resources on mastering a single area of our lives."
>
> —TONY ROBBINS

Good questions begin with:	Bad questions begin with:
What	Why
When	Can't I?
Where	
Who	
How	

Great job! The lists you've just generated in this section are the first step in targeting your problem areas and structuring your game plan. Keep your lists close at hand. (I keep mine in a journal in my purse, frequently looking at them to determine where I am in my life.) If you can easily access them, you can easily work on them—throughout the program and after!

Swan Secret: Write down one problem area on one page of your journal and carry it in your purse all week. When you're bored, pull it out and jot down any notes that come to you. With the added focus, you'll find all sorts of ideas popping into your head.

Nely G.

I was twenty-three with a perm, gapped teeth, and a Frida Kahlo unibrow. I had no self-confidence and no idea how to look and feel beautiful. At forty I have had my teeth fixed, lost the excess weight, finally plucked the eyebrows, and let my beautiful hair grow into its full potential. I got the boob lift that I always wanted after breast-feeding my son, and *The Swan's* Dr. Dubrow also performed lipo in the areas of my stomach and legs where exercise proved useless. I have been through therapy, career and life coaching, meditation workshops, and I've gone back to church. Even at my age, I was selected for *People* magazine's "Most Beautiful People" issue. I feel and am beautiful, at last.

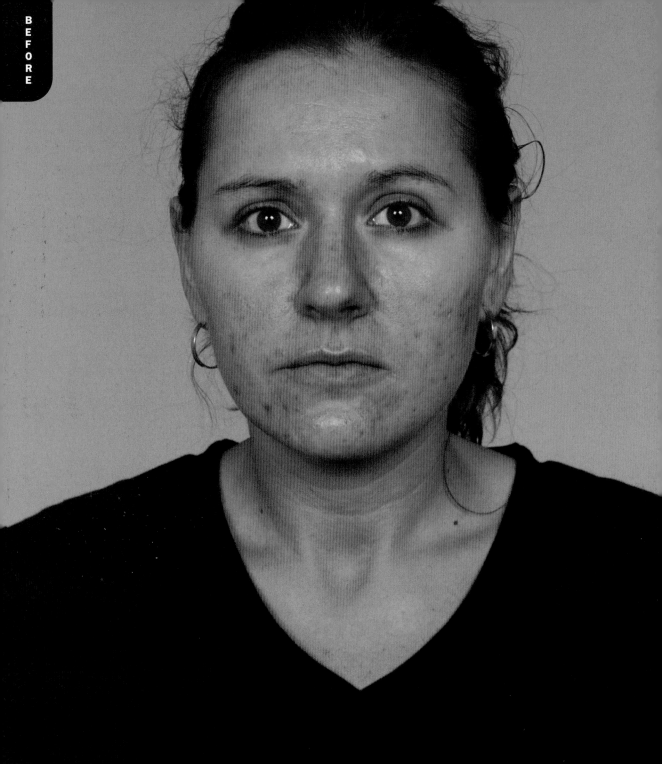

Andrea M. **Andrea struggled with the Curriculum and her self-esteem.**
Although she still has some work to do, she has truly made progress on the inside and out.

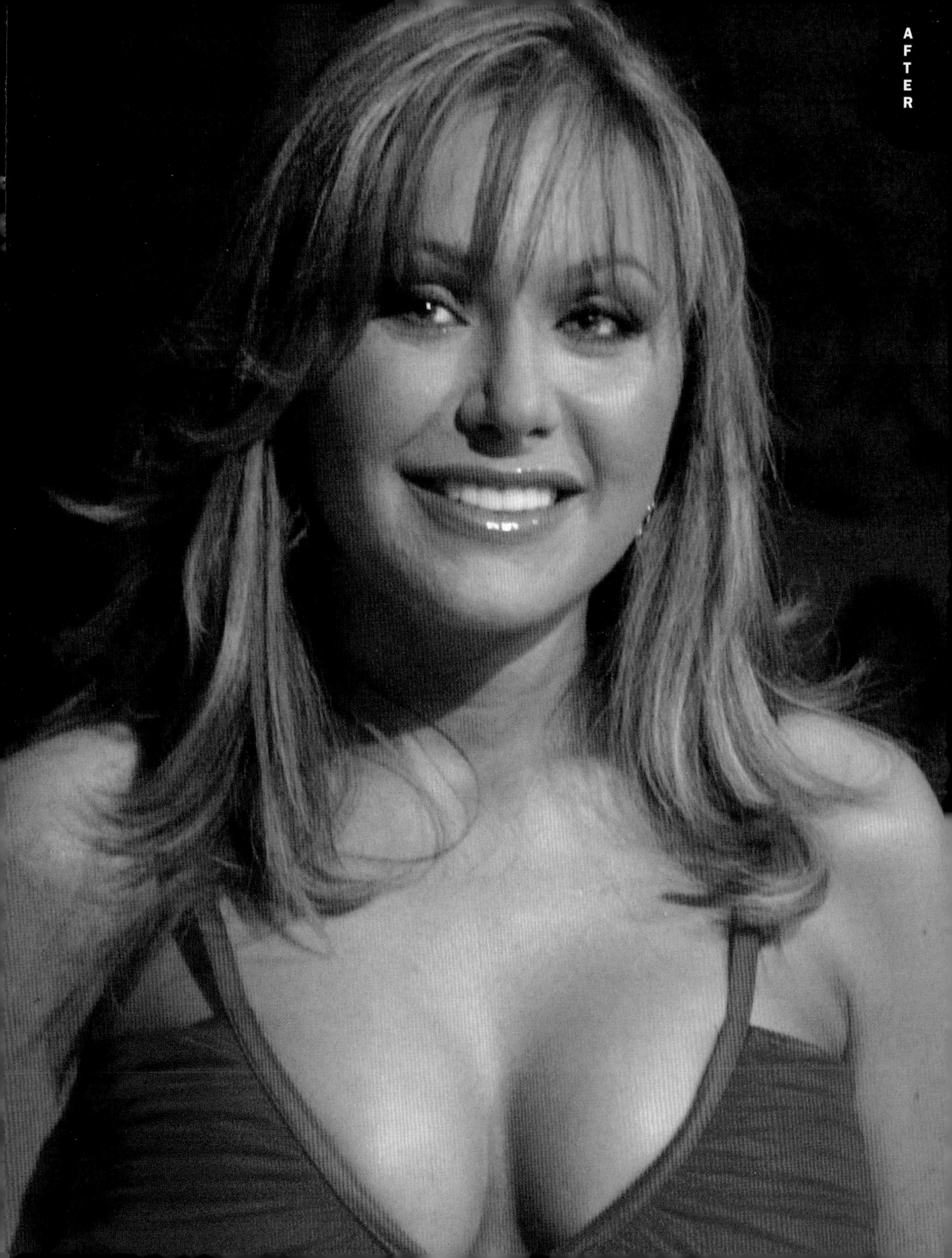
AFTER

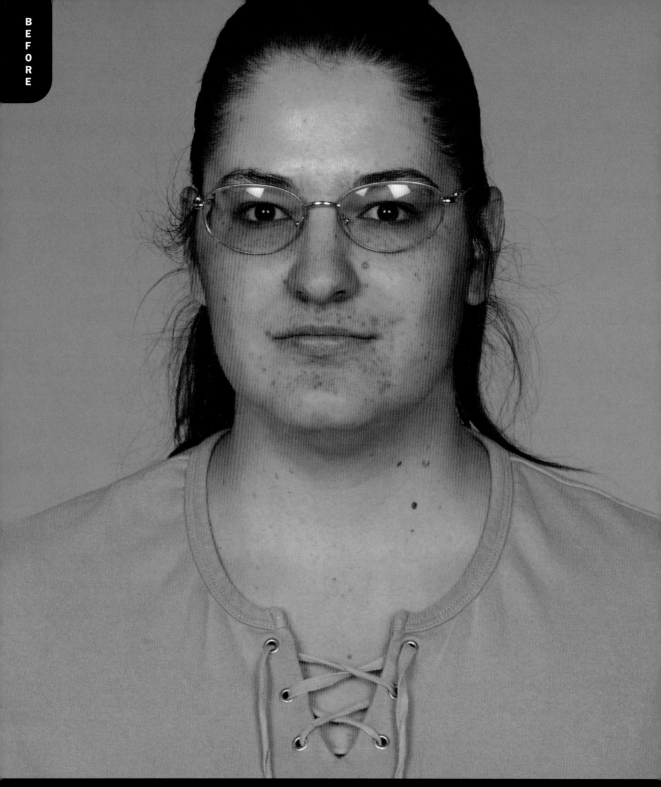

Belinda B. Belinda fully embraced the Curriculum and discovered that she's ready to make the transition in her career from nurse to doctor.

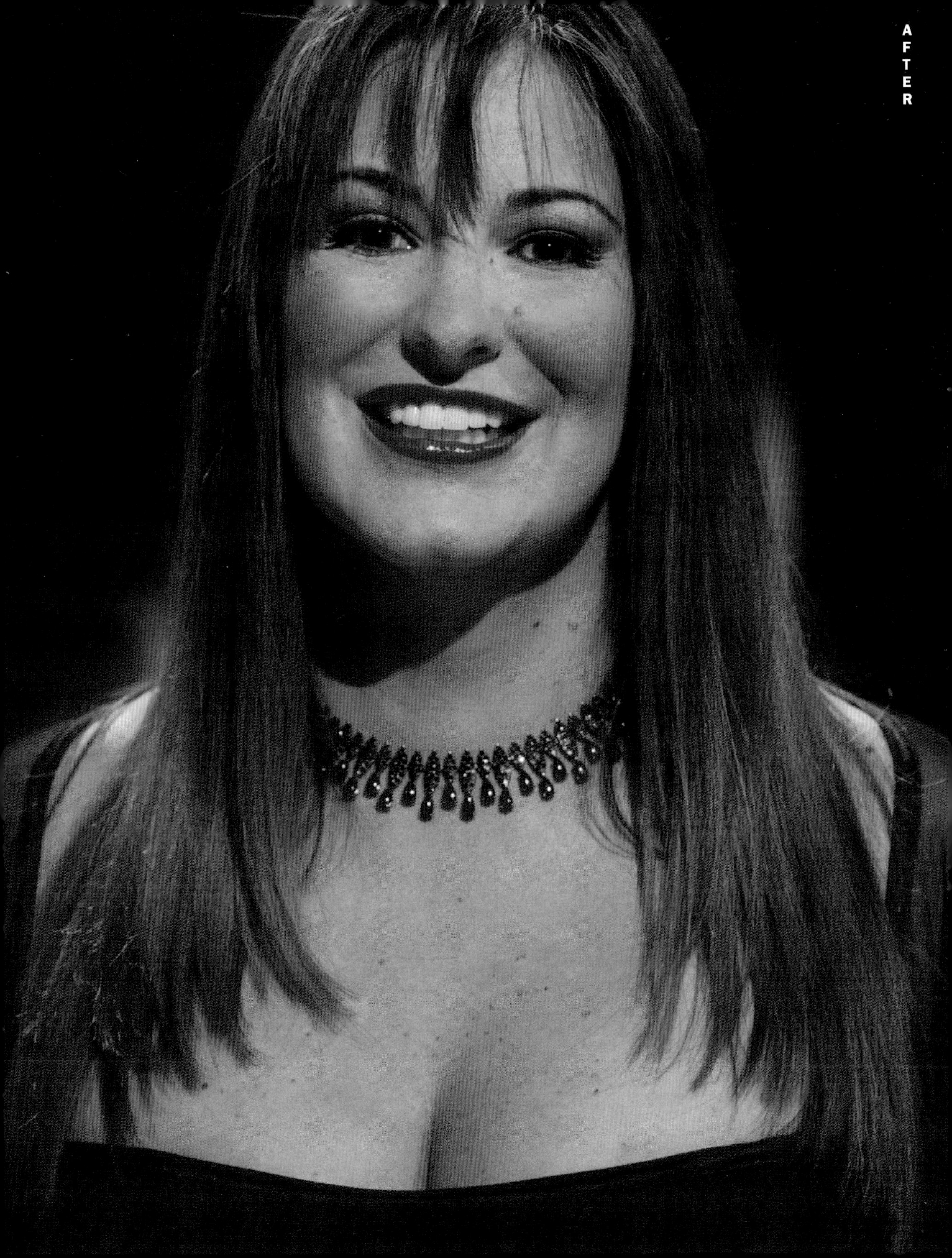
AFTER

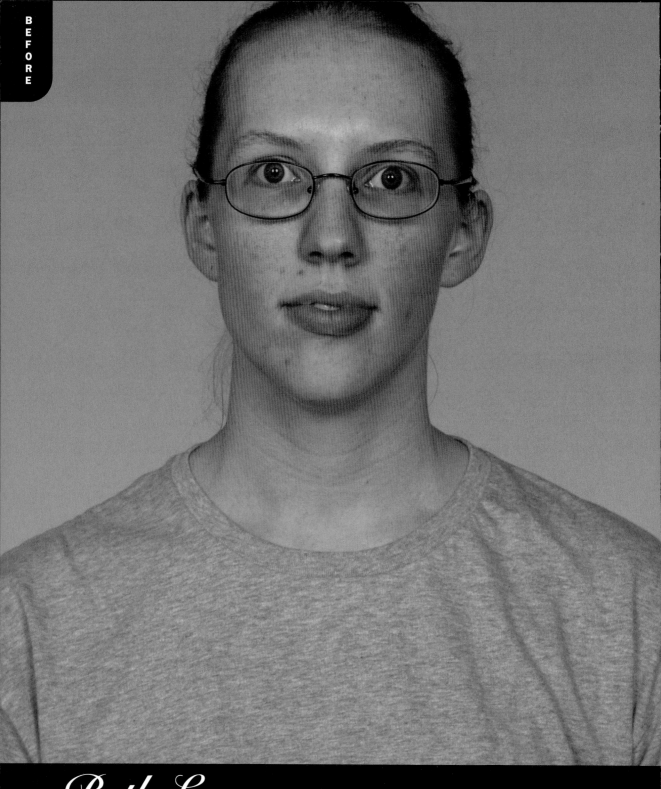

Beth L. **When she arrived, Beth was angry and insecure because her husband had kissed another woman. We did a lot of work to understand the dynamics of her marriage. She left confident and ready to play a stronger role in her relationship.**

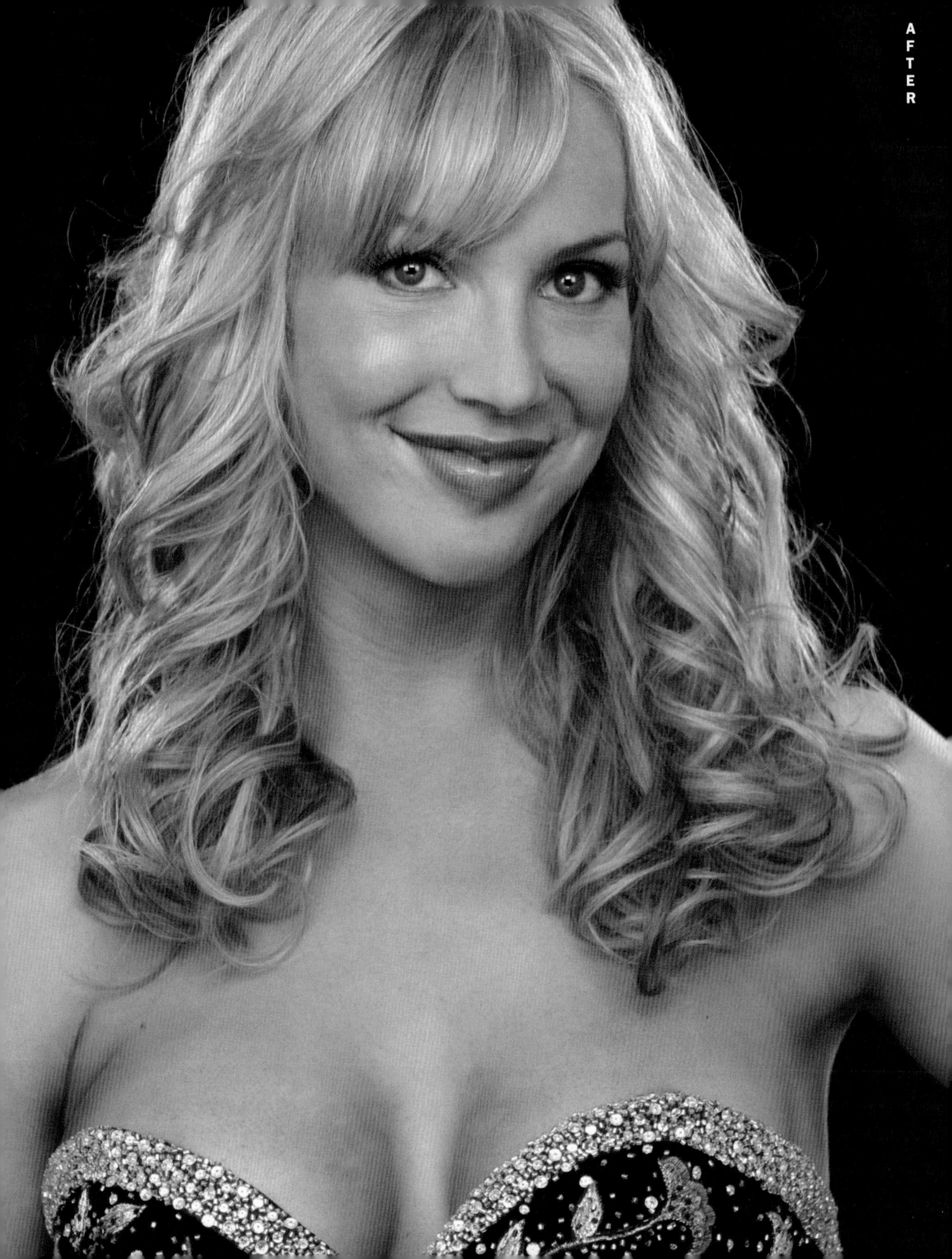
AFTER

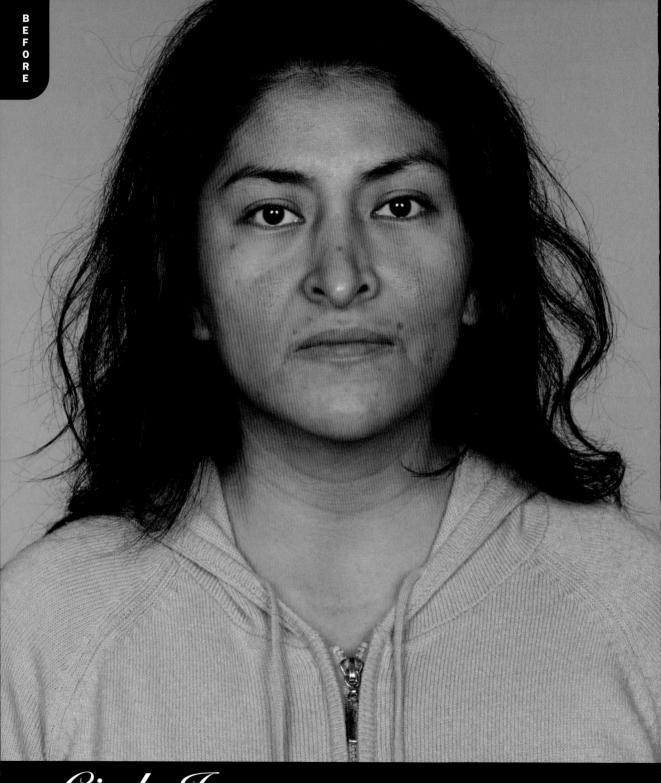

Cindy T. **Cindy was a self-proclaimed "witch." After a nose job and some in-depth work on the Curriculum, she left as a gorgeous, confident woman who finally feels good about her decision to be a stay-at-home mom.**

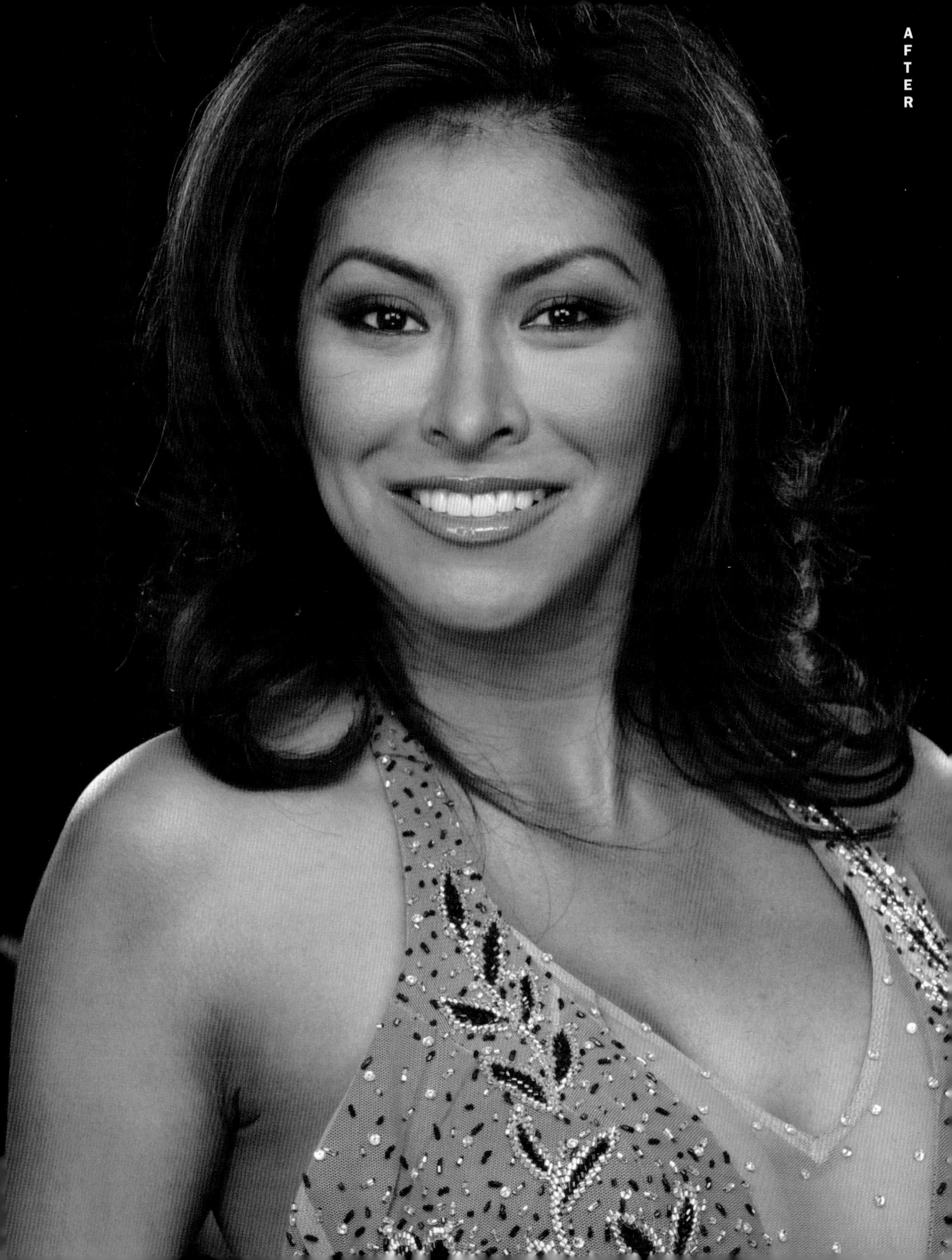
AFTER

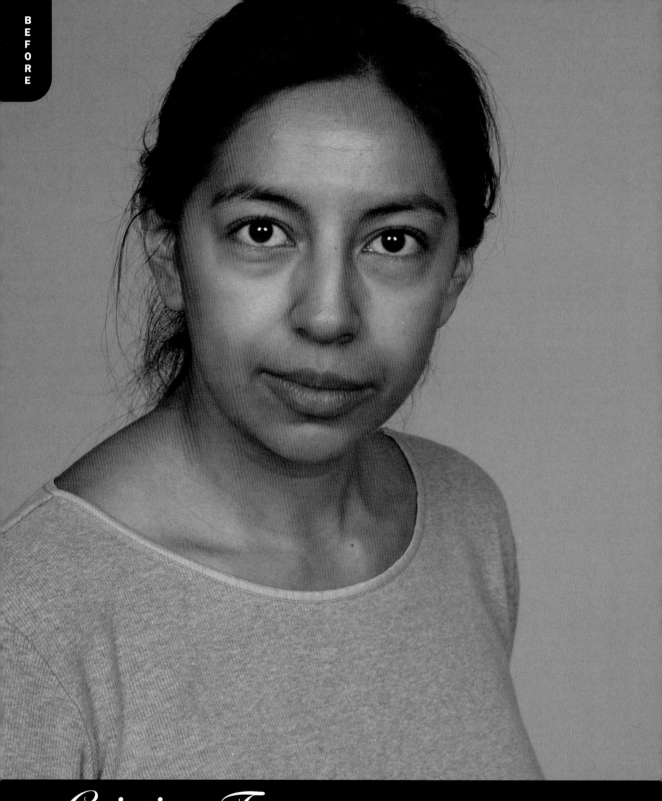

Cristina T. Cristina's life dream of becoming a belly dancer may come true! She
arrived terribly insecure about her body and her relationship. She left a sensual vixen.

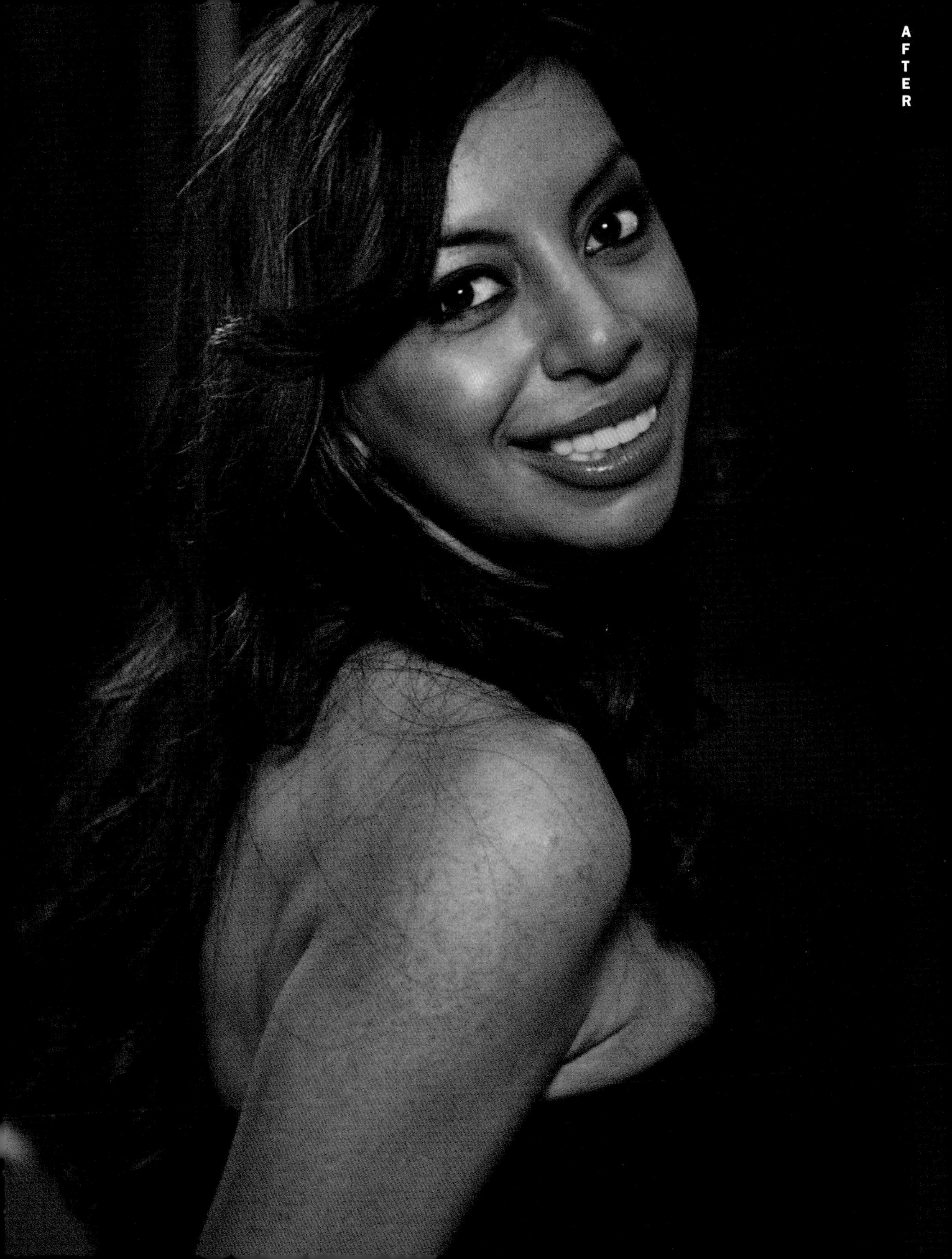

AFTER

Dawn G. **Dawn focused on managing her anger and renewing her femininity. She's now a**

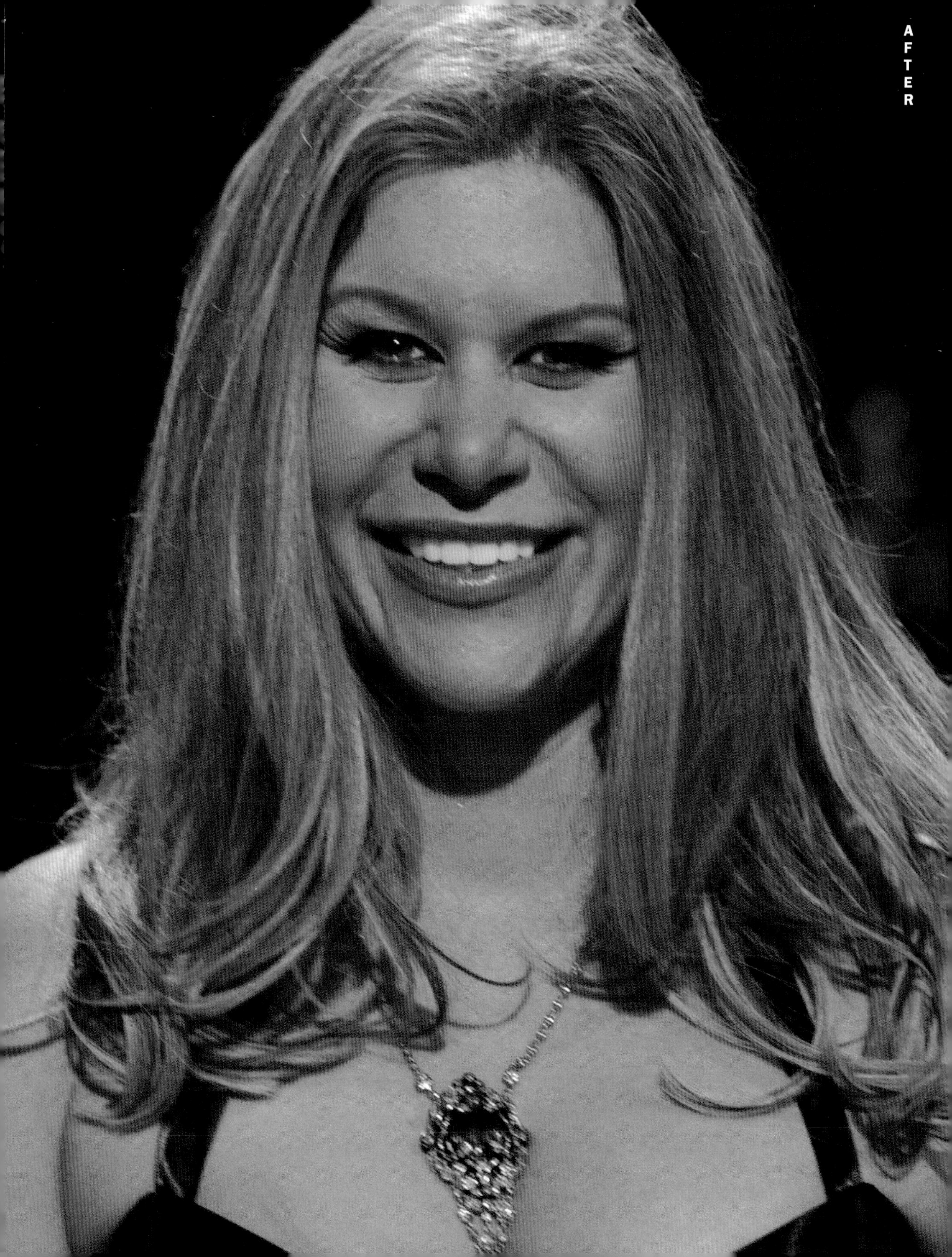
AFTER

Kathy R. Kathy arrived angry at the world and unconcerned about her looks. Though she had a tough time with the surgery, she worked hard to create the most unique look and personality I saw on the show.

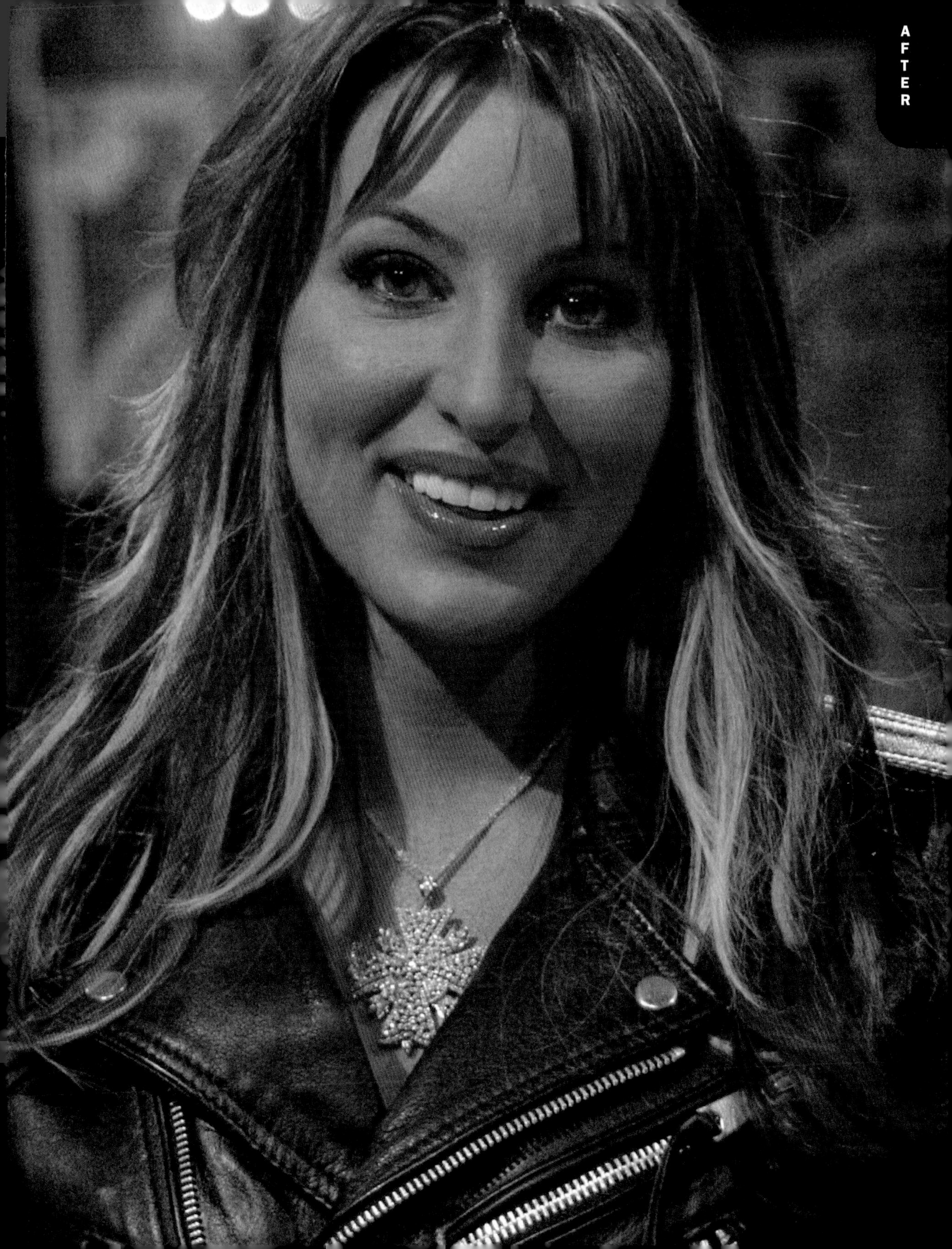

AFTER

Kelly A. Kelly arrived feeling unattractive and insecure and left looking like a bombshell. She still has work to do (she continues to focus too much on the negative), but has so much potential.

AFTER

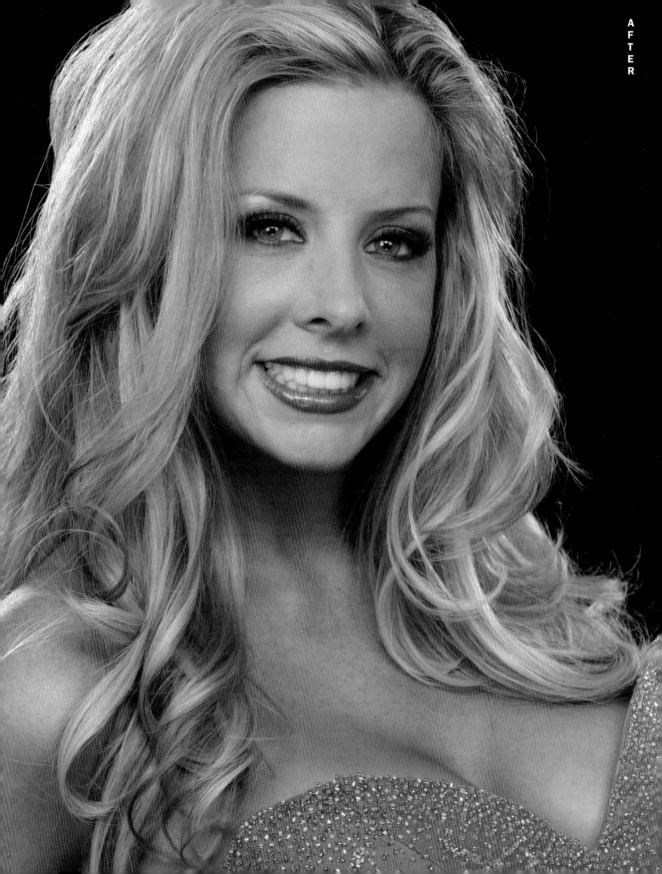

Kelly B. **Kelly was pretty when she arrived, so we worked mainly on her interior to help her find happiness. She left a beauty on the inside and out.**

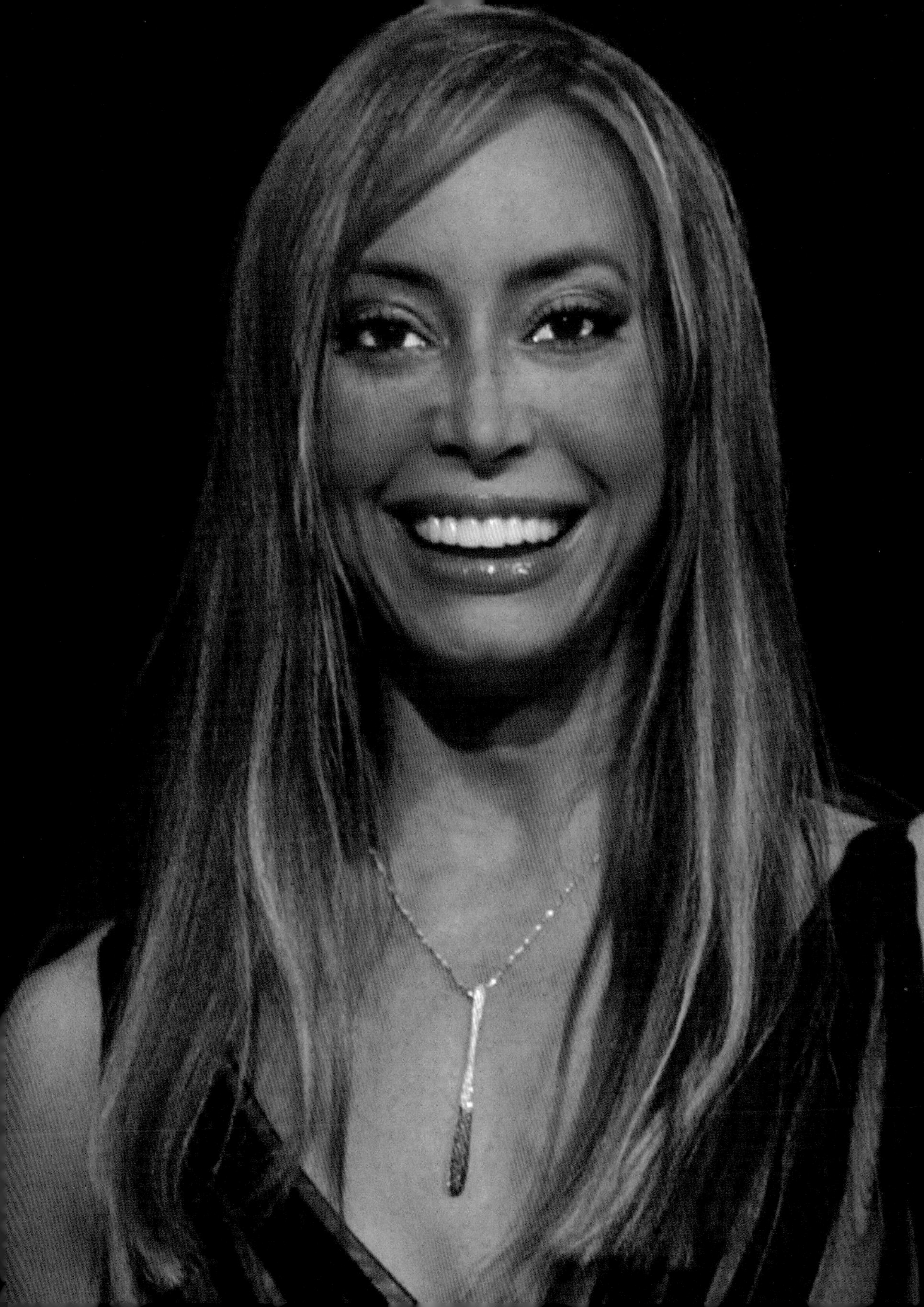

AFTER

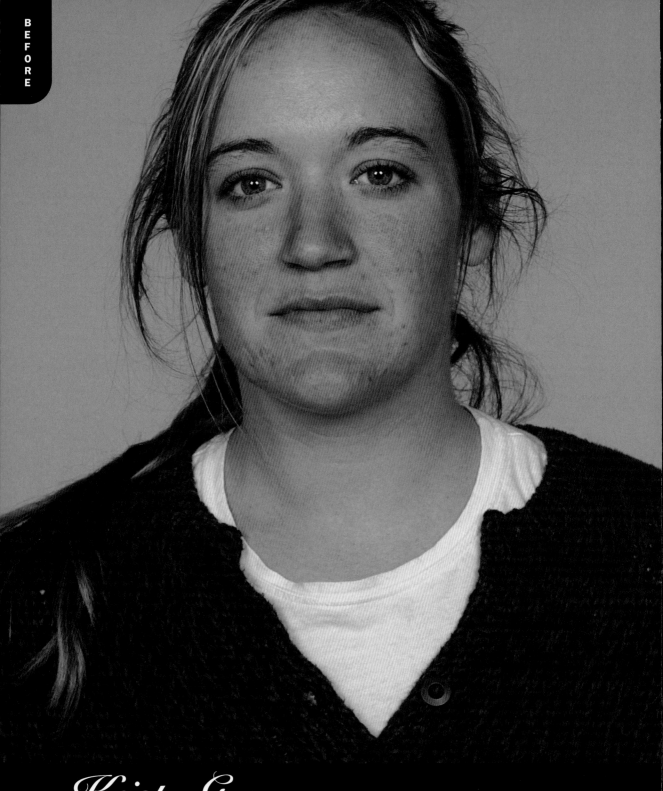

Kristy G. **Coming out of the military, Kristy was a take-charge woman who didn't know how to receive. We worked hard to mold her femininity and she left the show a truly sexy lady.**

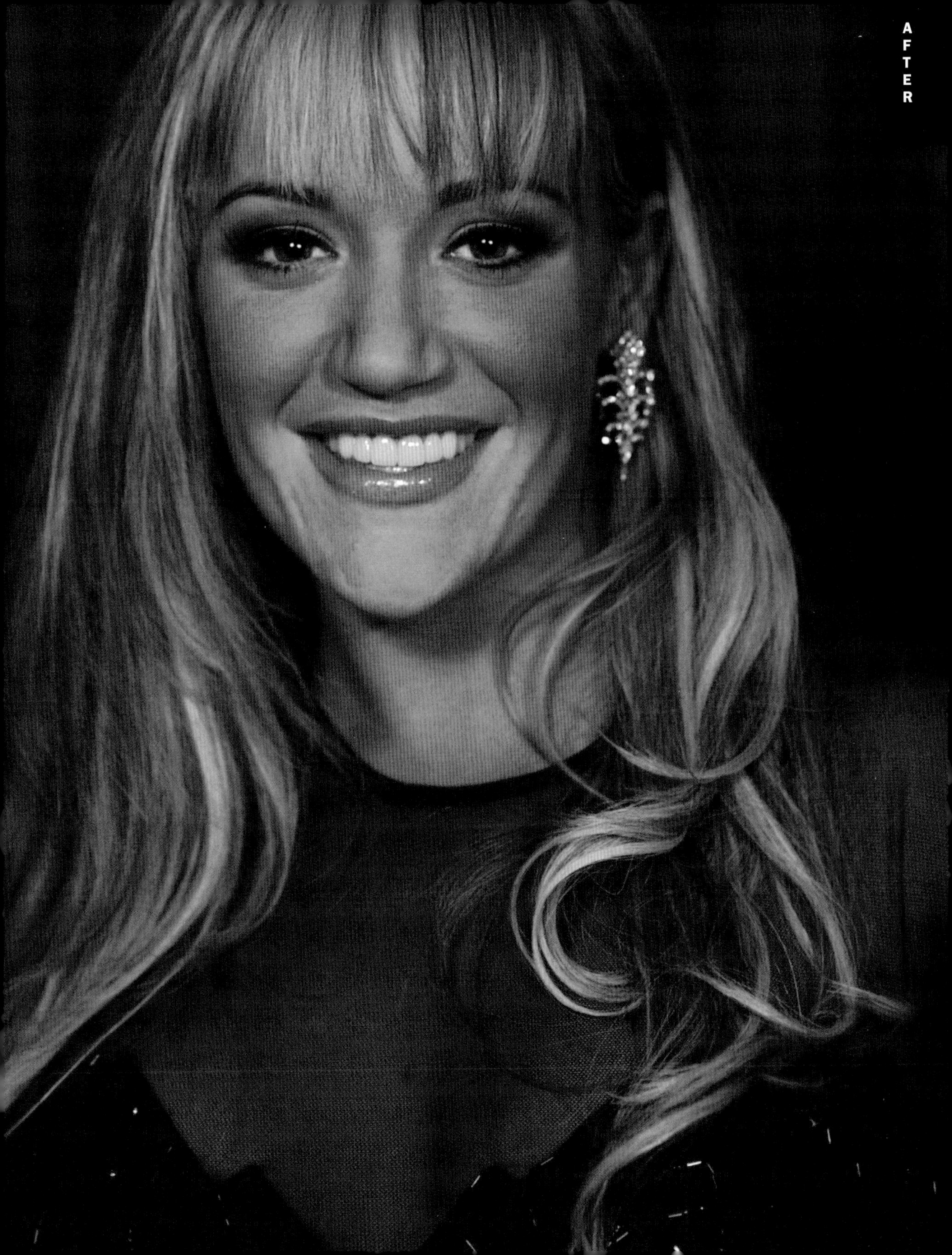
AFTER

Marnie R. **Marnie went from average to gorgeous. She still has a lot of work to do to overcome her depression, but after being without a date for ten years she's thrilled to report that men are sending her flowers.**

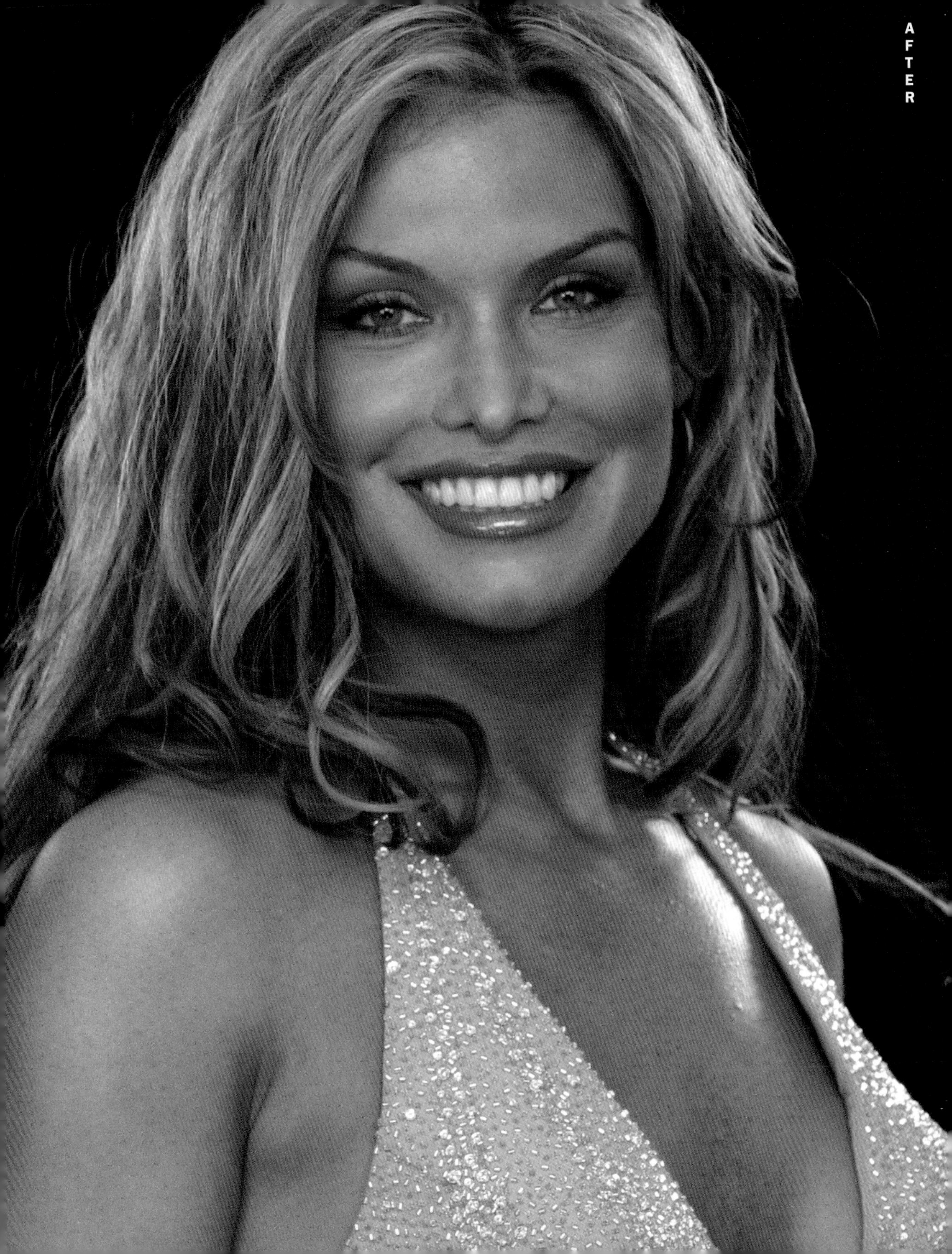

AFTER

Merline N. **Merline arrived with bad teeth and a bad attitude about her work as an interpreter for the deaf. Through the Curriculum, she realized that she has a unique skill set and endless possibilities. Today she can't stop smiling.**

AFTER

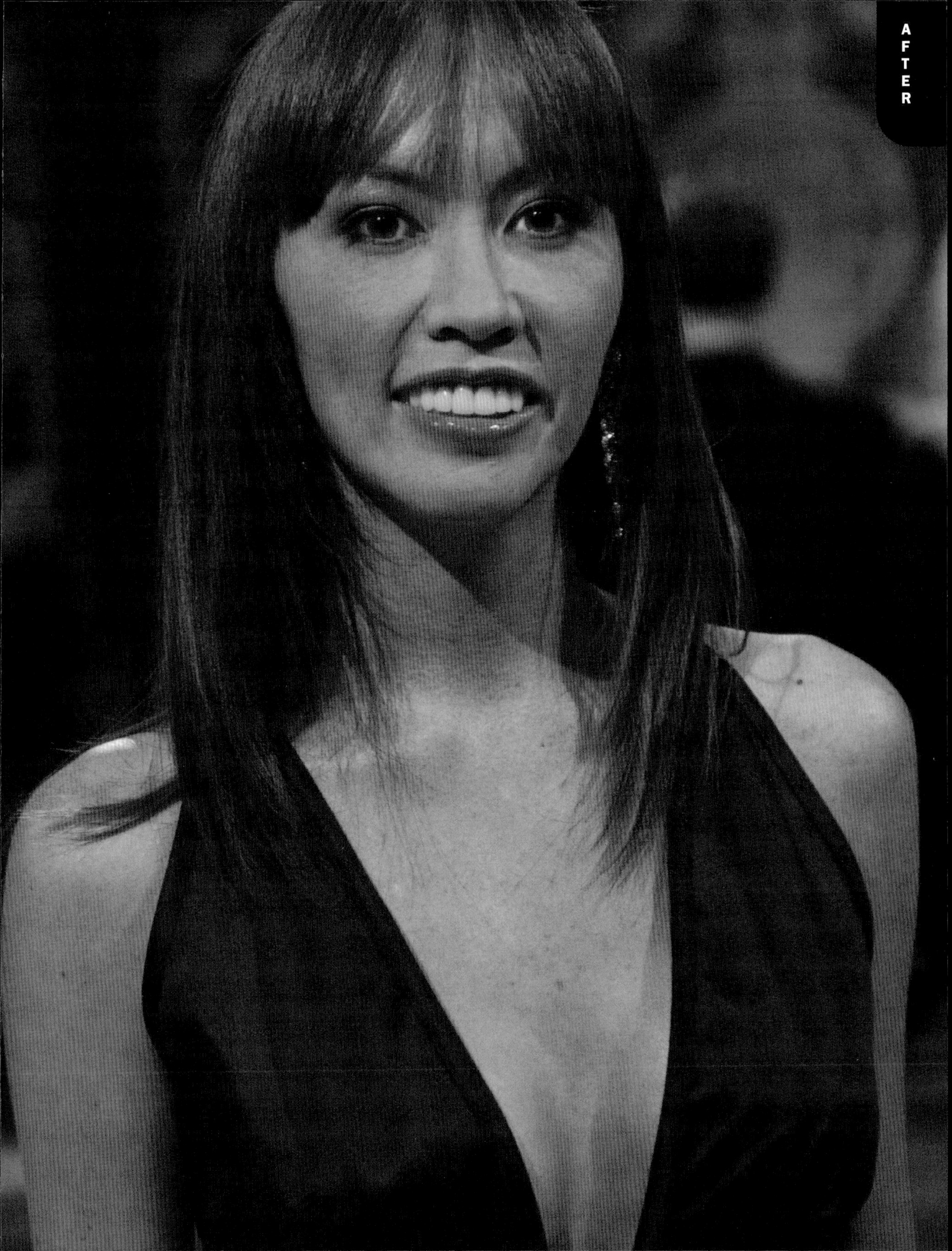

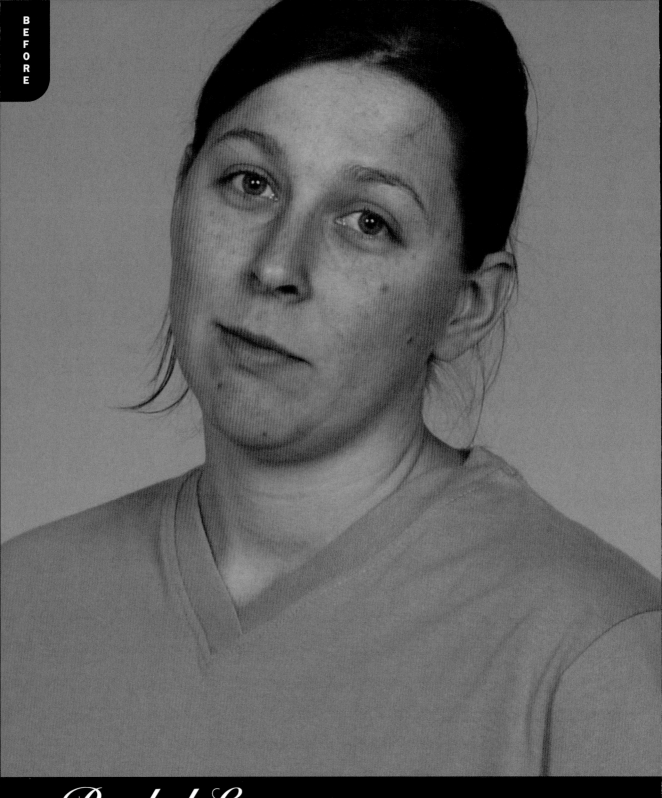

Rachel L.

Rachel surrendered to her transformation inside and out. She worked extremely hard and got the best results.

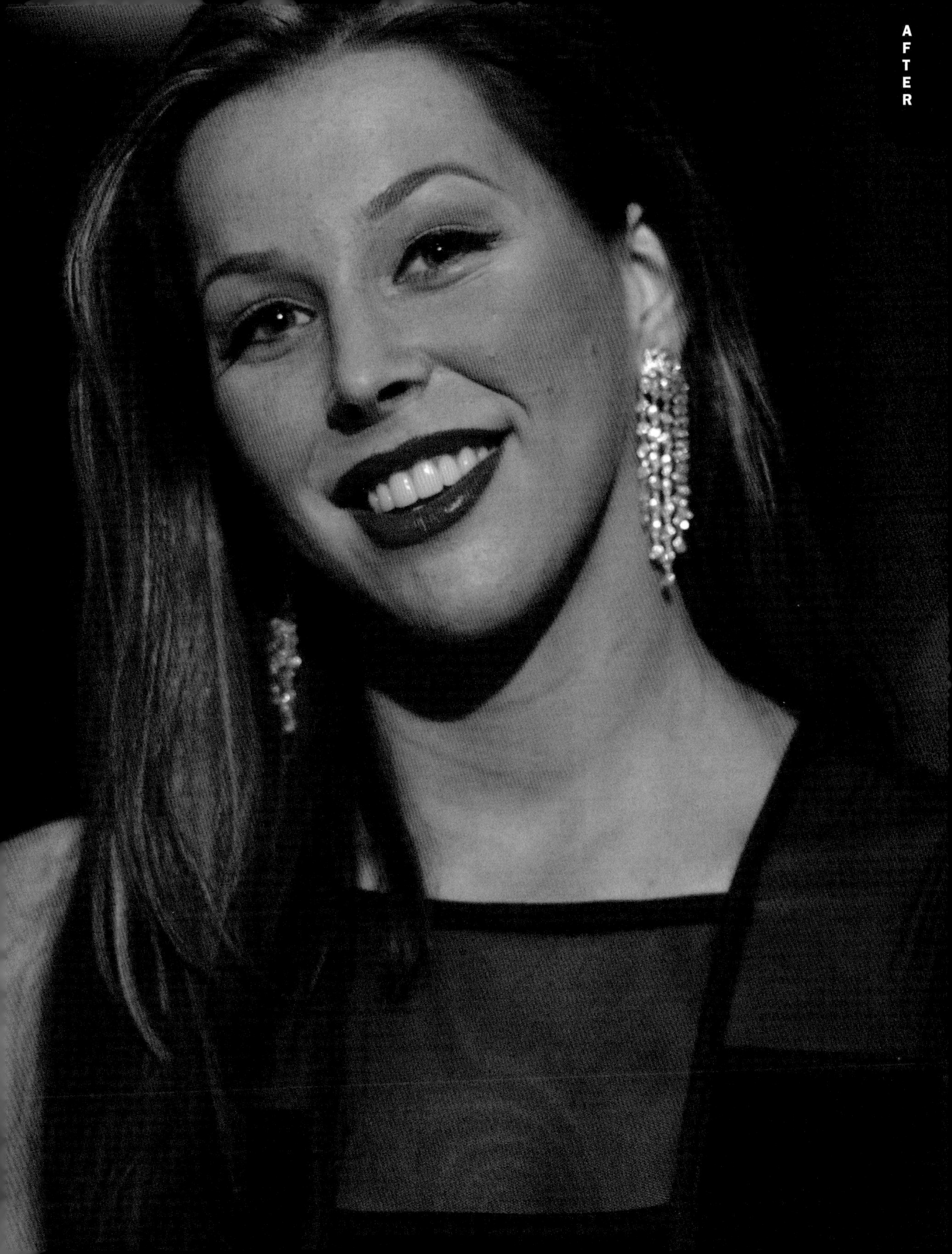
AFTER

Sarina V. **Sarina arrived still suffering from her divorce and unable to let go of her ex-husband. She left beautiful, but even more important, ready to move on with her life.**

AFTER

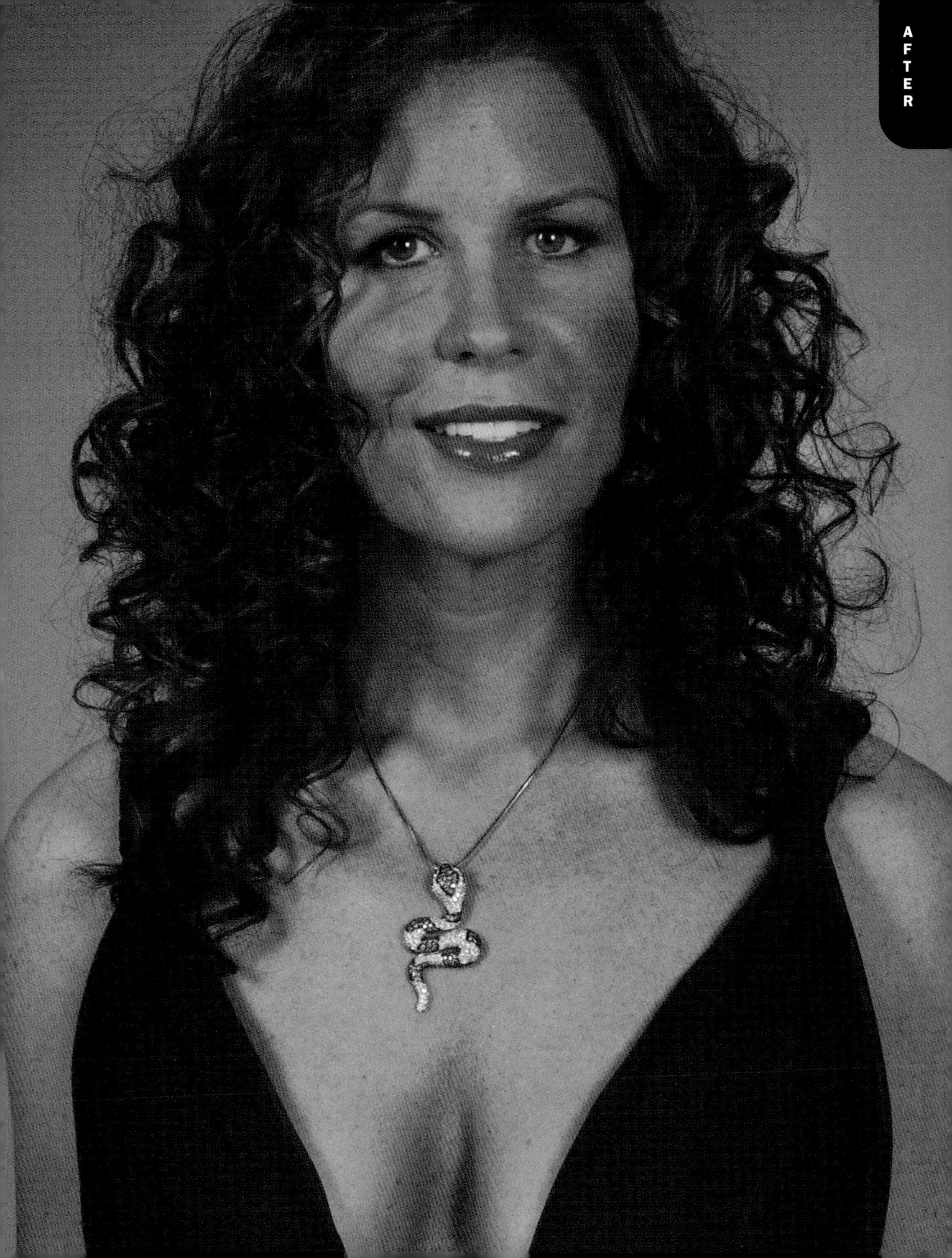

Tawnya C.

Tawnya used the Curriculum to blend her work and vocation.

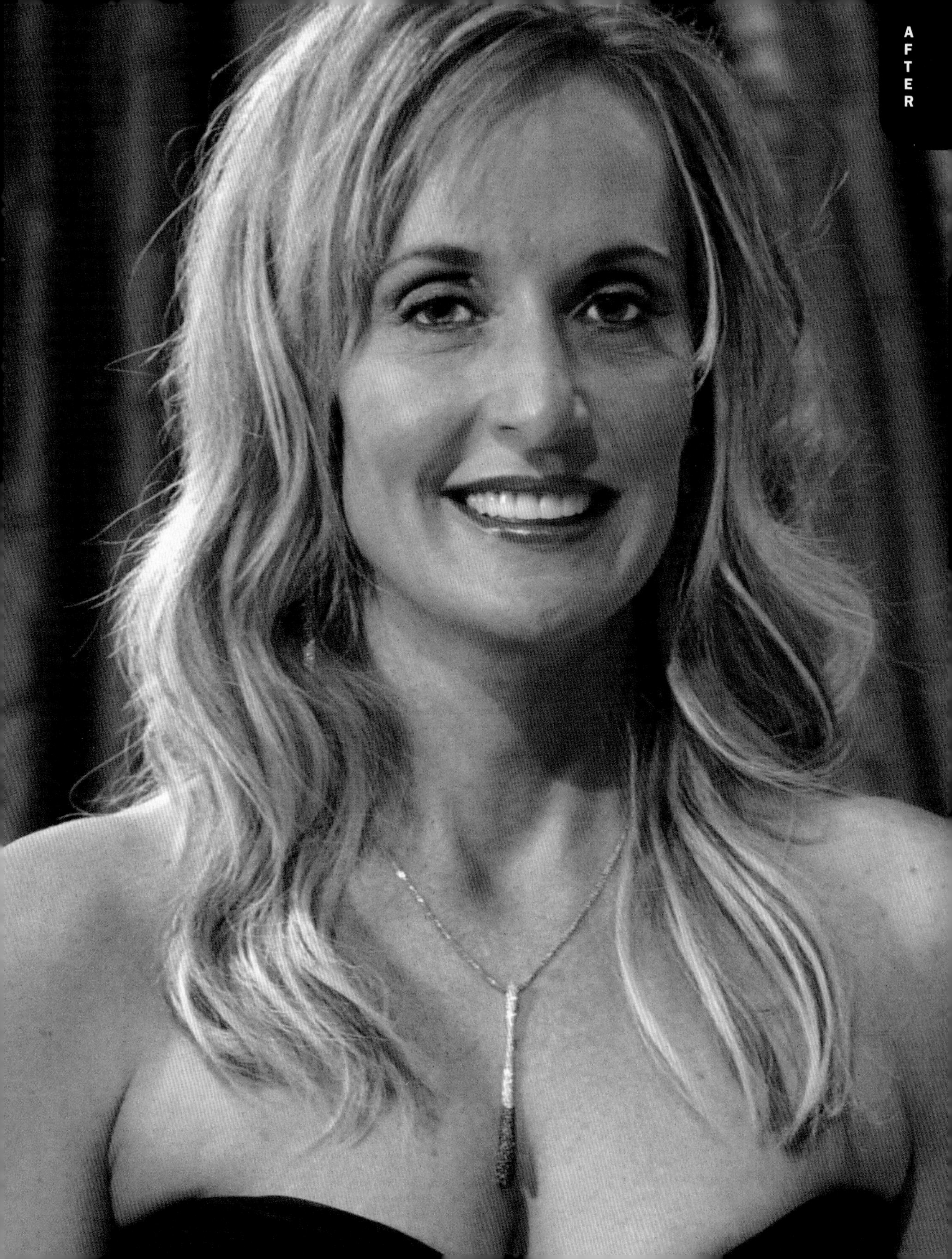
AFTER

This was one of the happiest moments of my life. I was thrilled to see Rachel, who felt so depressed and unattractive just four months before, turn into a deserving queen. Rachel went from a life stuck in a rut to the cover of *People* magazine, all through hard work, inside and out.

Find Your Muse

All the world's a stage
And all the men and women merely players:
They have their exits and their entrances;
And one [wo]man in [her] time plays many parts . . .

—WILLIAM SHAKESPEARE

In ancient Greek mythology, Zeus had nine enchanting daughters, the muses, who were the goddesses of artistic inspiration. Presiding over art, music, dancing, and history, they inspired all the masterpieces of the ancient world.

The muse is not confined to history. Look around you. You'll be amazed at the many men and women who can help inspire the masterpiece you will become!

Coveting Thy Neighbor's Success

Who are you jealous of?

Name of person: _____

"Successful people ask better questions and, as a result, they get better answers."

—TONY ROBBINS

If you supplied a name, give yourself one point. You're ahead of the game. Most of us will not answer this question the first time around. Why? Because it does not reflect well on us. It's negative. It's controversial. It suggests a dark side, and we're not supposed to be relishing our dark sides. Eight out of ten times, when I ask new Swans this question, they respond that, sure, they *admire* certain people, but are not jealous of anyone. Oh really?

"So when you watch the Academy Awards and you see Catherine Zeta Jones step out of her limousine, dripping in jewels, with her handsome husband on her arm, you don't feel a pit tightening in your stomach?" I ask.

"She's a movie star," they sigh. "It isn't the same."

"What if one of your friends was discovered by movie producers in the grocery store, and within a month she had a big contract worth a million dollars and a swanky apartment, and she was spotted frolicking on the beach with Tom Cruise? Any stomach pangs then?" Now I receive a shrug and a grunt. I'm making progress.

I understand the aversion. Jealousy is strictly discouraged in our culture. (If you lived through junior high school, you know why.) Unchecked, it is the most destructive energy in the universe. Expressions such as "the green-eyed monster" and "green with envy" paint the picture for you. Then of course there's the Tenth Commandment, which prohibits you from your neighbor's husband, her ox, or her Porsche. We are supposed to stifle jealousy and learn to be happy with what we have. That's the idea, anyway.

Unfortunately, as far as ideas go, this one isn't terribly insightful. When was the last time stifling anything made it go away? I'm here to offer you a new storyline: It's *okay* to covet. It's okay to be jealous. It's okay because it's *human.* As I learned from one of my spiritual mentors, Pema Chodron, a Tibetan Buddhist nun, acknowledging your darker impulses is an integral part of self-improvement.

As a Swan, you must recognize these negative feelings and use them to guide you along your path. After all, that which we are coveting is what we crave for ourselves, isn't it? This doesn't mean you have to broadcast your insecurities over a loudspeaker. No one but you needs to know who or what you envy. Confine the truth to this workbook, but set it free.

Who Knew Humanity Was So Well Read?

Shakespeare is probably to blame for first associating jealousy with green eyes in his play *The Merchant of Venice,* and for coining the term "green-eyed monster" in *Othello.* What he didn't mention was that green could be converted into a rainbow of possibility.

You signed the Swan Compact because you want more out of life. That commitment was an important accomplishment. The second step is identifying the people who have what you're after.

The Green-eyed Swan

Make a list of ten people who make your eyes glow like emeralds. You can list anyone—a movie star, a historical figure, a neighbor. Don't stop to analyze your reasons—just make the list and move on.

1. _____

2. _____

3. _____

4. _____

5. _____

6. _____

7. _____

8. _____

9. _____

10. _____

Good. Now, look at the names you came up with.

- Return to your list. Jot down some things you envy about each person next to their name. (e.g., beauty, relationship, career, confidence, poise, hair, etc.)

- What do the names on your list have in common? (i.e., Do they all have great bodies, happy marriages, or their own businesses?)_____

- Now, circle the words or phrases that reappear again and again. That repetition is your thread. A thread tells you what you're missing in your life. (My thread tends to be "marriage.") Write down your thread: _____

- Who on the list epitomizes this trait?_____ (name one person)

CONVERTING JEALOUSY INTO INSPIRATION

Now, let's say that while making your list you discovered that what you lack is a loving husband. (Okay, it's what I lack, but for argument's sake let's say it's you.) And you've identified Kate Hudson as the luckiest wife in the world. It doesn't matter that you don't actually know Kate Hudson, or that you can't confirm whether her marriage is exceptional enough to be jealous of it at all. As a celebrity, she is a fantasy, and in large part a Hollywood creation. Why not use her to inspire your imagination and fire up your motivation?

Musing is less about truth, you see, than about perception; it tells you absolutely nothing about Kate Hudson, but it reveals a great deal about *you*.

Kate Hudson's Perfect Marriage Habits

Let's take the fantasy Kate Hudson and figure out how she has accomplished the perfect marriage. To do this, we must first identify the areas of her life that are relevant to her relationship. Let's do a little brainstorming.

I. LIST THE AREAS OF KATE'S LIFE THAT ARE PERTINENT:

    a. Beauty? Yes.

    b. Spirituality? Perhaps.

    c. Fun? Yes.

    d. Education? Yes.

II. NOW, ADDRESS EACH AREA WITH A SPECIFIC QUESTION.

    a. Area: Beauty

    Question: What would Kate do to maintain and/or accentuate her beauty?

1. Would she get facials regularly? Yes.
2. Would she cut her own hair over the bathroom sink? No.
3. Would she work out regularly? Yes. How often? At least five times a week—with a trainer.
4. Would Kate have bad gums? No.
5. Would she go to the dentist twice a year? Yes.
6. Would she see a gynecologist regularly? Yes.
7. Would she visit a therapist if she had an emotional problem? Yes.

> "In truth, the only difference between those who have failed and those who have succeeded lies in the difference of their habits."
>
> —OG MANDINO, SELF-HELP GURU

b. Area: Fun

Question: How does Kate find joy in her life?

  1. Does Kate find time for friends in her busy schedule? Yes.

  2. Does she get away for a weekend with her husband? Yes.

III. NEXT, COMPARE KATE'S HABITS TO YOURS.

Mark every practice of hers that has eluded you with an X.

I know what you're thinking: "Of course Kate Hudson can do all these things; she's rich!" While you're correct on that front, the truth is that you, too, can afford all of these things if you prioritize and find services offered at a price that works for you. Look online and in newspapers for discounts, ask friends with unique expertise for help, use those coupons left on your car and your door.

Muse Habit Workshop

Get the picture? Now you try.

  1. Your issue: _____

  2. Your muse: _____

  3. Circle the following areas of his/her life relevant to this issue: love, health and fitness, family and friends, work, vocation, community, education, forgiveness, sex, spirituality, fun, and beauty.

  4. For each area you circled, write up four questions for your muse.

      a. Area of life: _____

          Question 1: _____   *Answer:* _____

          Question 2: _____   *Answer:* _____

          Question 3: _____   *Answer:* _____

          Question 4: _____   *Answer:* _____

b. Area of life: _____

    Question 1: _____   *Answer:* _____

    Question 2: _____   *Answer:* _____

    Question 3: _____   *Answer:* _____

    Question 4: _____   *Answer:* _____

c. Area of life: _____

    Question 1: _____   *Answer:* _____

    Question 2: _____   *Answer:* _____

    Question 3: _____   *Answer:* _____

    Question 4: _____   *Answer:* _____

d. Area of life: _____

    Question 1: _____   *Answer:* _____

    Question 2: _____   *Answer:* _____

    Question 3: _____   *Answer:* _____

    Question 4: _____   *Answer:* _____

Muse and the Masterpiece

Artists from Dante to Shakespeare to Picasso found inspiration for their masterpieces in local muses. A young woman named Beatrice Portinari has been called Dante's greatest muse; Shakespeare addresses a mysterious "Muse" in many of his sonnets; and Pablo Picasso found inspiration in the beautiful, rebellious brunette named Dora Maar, who figures in many of his paintings, including *The Weeping Woman*.

5. What is your muse doing that you are not, with respect to each quality/aspiration? List the habits here:

i. _____

ii. _____

iii. _____

iv. _____

v. _____

vi. _____

vii. _____

viii. _____

ix. _____

x. _____

xi. _____

xii. _____

Musing a Real Person

One night I was over at the Swan apartments and the girls and I were discussing jealousy. This wasn't the first time we'd addressed the topic, but that night the women were as responsive as stones. I prodded and prodded, and finally, with a refreshing burst of venom, one Swan admitted: "You know, I get really jealous when Kelly gets letters from her boyfriend. He's so loving, and I've never had that."

"What's the lesson?"

"That I hate Kelly?" the Swan offered.

I made a suggestion. "Instead of hating someone, you need to say, 'I will not settle for anything less than a man who does these things for me.'"

You see, Kelly mastered something her fellow Swan has not, and in order to take advantage of the opportunity before her, the jealous Swan needs to acknowledge it and learn everything she can about Kelly's relationship. Kate Hudson is one thing. She'll inspire you to strive, and she'll help you collect data about yourself. But if your muse is in the same room, you can do a whole 'nother kind of data collection.

"We can't solve problems by using the same kind of thinking we used when we created them."

—ALBERT EINSTEIN

"Wanting something is not enough; you must hunger for it. Your motivation must be absolutely compelling in order to overcome the obstacles that will invariably come your way."

—LES BROWN

REAL MUSE RESOURCE

If you've found a local muse—a friend or someone in your community, someone *accessible*—you've got a valuable resource. Don't let her get away. Sit down with her and learn everything she knows about your subject. I've been unable to find the right man, for example, so whenever I meet someone in a great relationship, I try to think of her as a *resource*. I go out of my way to ask for information I can use: *How did you meet? What attracted you to each other? What do you disagree about?* And so on. Meeting with a muse is a great way to begin compiling data on your subject. And it will make her feel good. She has something you covet, and you're showing her that you admire her for it.

A Penny (or a Free Lunch) for Your Thoughts

Write down one accessible muse, someone with whom you can sit down and discuss your subject (feel free to jot down other possibilities in the margin if you'd like). If he or she is a friend, there's no need to tell her you're doing research; people love to talk about themselves. If she's an acquaintance but not someone you know well enough to call your friend, arrange a lunch date to pick her brain, and make sure to mention that it's on you. Most people will do anything for a free lunch, trust me. Over the years, I've spent thousands on lunches—and it was money well-spent.

_____

MUSE'S NAME

_____

EXPERTISE

Becoming Your Muse

Now that you've identified some muses and what they can teach you, you can begin to implement their winning behavior into your life. Active musing comes in tremendously handy when you're looking to adopt characteristics you weren't necessarily born with.

Take me. I spend a significant amount of my time in rooms with very big business moguls, asking for money. In fact, in the television business, I have a reputation for being able to ask anybody for millions of dollars and getting it. This quality amazes my friends and coworkers, but the truth is that I wasn't born with it. You see, when I enter those big chilly rooms and take my seat across from Rupert Murdoch, I am not Nely Galán, immigrant Cuban. I am an older Jewish man named Mel.

Allow me to explain. I was raised to be a good Catholic girl, to be humble, and to believe that money is not important—and even if it were, that I don't deserve it. Mel, however, possessed none of these concerns and was—in my eyes at least—the quintessential businessman. His position was always very simple: Take the plunge.

The first time I entered a mogul's room, I left Nely in the car. I straightened my imaginary red tie and listened as Mel's gravelly voice rattled around in my brain: "If ya don't ask for a lotta money, they're not gonna take the deal seriously. Little lady, they're no better than you are. It's just as hard to ask for five million as it is to ask for five thousand. I'll be ashamed if you don't ask for the money."

Mel was right, of course. I asked and I received. After that, whenever I found myself in a situation I believed Mel could handle better than me, I straightened my imaginary tie. Mel went into those meetings and got the millions Nely Galán did not feel comfortable asking for, but it was *Nely* who left with the cash.

The best part about musing? Over the years I've assumed Mel's identity so many times that I don't have to pretend I'm him anymore. If I'm in a room with moguls, I *am* him. I have no shame in asking for money these days—once you've taken the plunge four times, the fifth time is *notta problem*. At least, that's what Mel would say.

Benjamin Franklin Mused, Too

In his *Autobiography,* Benjamin Franklin mentions making a list of thirteen qualities he valued in others and organizing them in a notebook in order of importance. He then wrote one quality on a single page and focused on it for an entire week, hoping to become a little bit more like the men he held in high regard.

Being Mel

Identify one situation that gives you anxiety. It could be giving a presentation, hosting a dinner party, socializing with a group of new people, or going on a job interview.

_____

_____

In a few sentences, explain what about this situation makes you uncomfortable. For example, what are your fears? What is your goal? What are the obstacles? Be specific.

_____

_____

_____

Identify a muse for the situation. Who would pull off that situation marvelously?

_____

In a few sentences, explain how this person would excel in the situation.

_____

_____

_____

Reread the above, and examine the components of your muse's winning behavior (e.g., dress, confidence, what he or she might say to accomplish the task, etc.). Create the scene. What would your muse say? How would he/she behave? What would he/she wear? Etc.

_____

_____

_____

_____

_____

"We ask ourselves, 'Who am I to be brilliant, gorgeous, talented and fabulous?' Actually, who are you not to be?"

—MARIANNE WILLIAMSON

MASTERING THE MUSE

Though it may be uncomfortable at first, active musing is no insignificant exercise on the path to Swan salvation—it is one of the most important steps to success, so you have to start getting comfortable with the idea. After all, how are you going to transform yourself if you don't know what you want to become?

I muse any time I feel uneasy about an approaching situation. Going to a premiere, for example, is very uncomfortable for me, because I'm not a style person. But honey, I can do it, because I make believe I'm an actress. And then I think, *Of course I'm going to hire a hair and makeup person and a stylist. That's what they would do. Am I worth less than an actress?*

Of course, musing doesn't always mean a wholesale rip-off of someone's behavior or look. Sometimes, you have to be a little more creative. For instance, I have had many muses in the business world. One, Chris Albrecht, my boss at HBO, was the best salesman I ever saw, and I knew that I could learn a lot from him. Above all, he was a storyteller. Chris would go into a meeting, tell a hilarious story, and have the entire conference room cracking up by the time he got to his pitch. He managed to sell his ideas without their noticing! It was brilliant.

When preparing for my own pitches, I figured out ways to use Chris's approach to break the ice. I wasn't a comedian, so I used my outfit as a distraction to get the room's attention. I'd enter a room with bells jingling, literally, wearing the loudest colors and fabrics I could find. They weren't outfits, they were costumes. But people in the room always seemed to love them; I was memorable, and my act broke the ice. To this day I'm always running into people who stop me and begin with, "Hey, Nely, remember that wacky outfit you wore to that meeting at Universal?"

This Week's Lesson

Jealousy is no errant human quality—it exists to tell you everything you need to know about yourself and your desires. It is the mirror you hold up to your developing self and your guide along the path to transformation. Use it and you have the power to become anyone you want.

Swan Secret: Embrace your green eyes—they improve your vision.

Work

What Do You Do to Make Money?

"What do you like about your work?" I was talking to a blackjack dealer who complained about the long hours, low pay, and repetitive nature of her work.

"Nothing," she said.

"Not a thing?" I suppose she thought that would be the end of it. But I don't let anyone off so easily. "Do you know how to count numbers really fast because of your job?"

She agreed that this was true.

"And do you know how to size up a client really quickly because of your work?"

She admitted to being an unusually keen judge of character.

"What about fringe benefits?"

She mentioned something about free massages. In fact, before we were through, she'd compiled a list of about twenty "bonuses" she'd initially overlooked. This didn't mean she liked her job. It meant she was beginning to recognize its impact on her life.

I am not here to convince you to remain in a job you hate. This chapter is about looking at the larger picture, about fact-finding, *not* resolution. We'll get to resolution in due course. Our current objective is simply to help you unearth the skills you've developed, to help you chart your professional likes and dislikes, and to help you find that all-important unifying thread that will direct you to the next step.

Appreciate Your Unique Trajectory

Like everyone else, I've worked a lot of less than ideal jobs in my life, but those jobs got me where I am today. My first job, for example, was at The Limited. I was only fifteen, but I quickly understood that I was a saleswoman at heart. Of course, I also realized that there were a lot of things about working in the sales department of a clothing store that I didn't like. I hated doing inventory and replacing clothes on their shelves. Part of the reason I didn't like that aspect of the job, I understand now, is that I am what you might call "anal organized." I spent unnecessary hours perfecting the look of the shelves and the position of shirt collars.

After that, I got myself a guest editorship at *Seventeen* magazine. This time I knew I had found my calling. I loved magazines. I loved writing stories (I'd gotten the job offer after submitting an article). At *Seventeen*, I learned a ton of things I would use in later jobs. I became skilled at performing research on any subject. I learned how to make the pieces of a project come together. I began to understand what it meant to gratify an audience and to meet hard deadlines. I also realized that my fashion sense was cheeseball tacky (something I would learn again and again before I did anything about it). Even more important to my professional trajectory, I discovered that the magazine world is populated by rich girls who don't need to make money. I am the daughter of Cuban immigrants; I need to make money. Though a great learning experience, this job was ultimately not for me.

We tend to forget that everything we do leads us to the next place. If you feel hopeless because you're stuck in a job you dislike, you aren't looking at the big picture. If you step out of things, you'll see where you're going, and why each job is simply one step toward your ultimate destination. I hadn't found my calling by my second job (or my third, fourth, or fifth), but the puzzle was coming together. By the time I left *Seventeen,* I was able to inventory what I'd picked up so far: *I'm good at sales. I like fashion but I won't starve for it. I like magazines but not as a career.* I was getting somewhere, and knowing that helped me to keep going.

One of the best things I did for myself when I was feeling stuck in a job was to draw up a chronological chart (see page 30) tracing all the positions I'd had over my career. Together, they gave me a tangible map, showing me precisely where I was heading all along.

JOB	LIKES	DISLIKES	SKILLS ACQUIRED
The Limited	Selling	Doing inventory	Selling / being organized
Seventeen	Glamorous job / storytelling / researching	No money	Researching / thinking on my feet
Teen TV Reporter	Traveling / interviewing interesting people / being on TV	Making no money / bus travel / bad hotels / finding myself in dangerous situations	Adapting to diverse circumstances and people / technical skills / teamwork / storytelling
News Producer, CBS	Action-packed job / seeing my work on air every day / diverse subject matter / challenging	Depressing subject matter / rushed schedule / factory mentality / rough lifestyle	Performing on short deadlines / making shows on low-budgets / understanding importance of keeping up with current events / editing
TV Station Manager	Being the top dog / community work / Hispanic market / dealing with advertisers	More technical than creative / long hours / managing a lot of people	Running a business / math / giving consumers what they want / realizing the importance of profit
Launched TV channels in Latin America (for Fox, HBO, Fox Kids, MGM, Sony)	Comfortable in Latin America, pioneering new markets / making good money / very creative	Continual travel / being out of the loop with U.S. peers	Making multiple businesses profitable / understanding how to do business in foreign markets / creating client lists / problem solving in foreign territory

JOB	LIKES	DISLIKES	SKILLS ACQUIRED
Telemundo, President	Using all my skills / creative / getting to work on things that mattered to me / Hispanic market / making lots of money	Too corporate / too many meetings / too much pressure	Understanding that I should be an entrepreneur and work for myself / learned to dress
Galán Entertainment, Founder / President	Creating a company in my own vision / making a lot of money / having my son come to work	Knowing that all revenue of the company is on me / not having the resources of a big company	Realized that sales, creativity and finance are keys to running a business.
The Swan	Truly the subject matter that interests me / using all my skills from previous jobs / combining creativity and business	Nothing	Culmination of everything I've done / I am uniquely prepared for this opportunity

CONCLUSION

In drawing up my chart, I discovered that when it comes to work, I have five non-negotiables:

1. I need to work for myself.

2. I need to work in television—it's a skill I've developed over 20 years.

3. The subject matter must reflect my vocation.

4. I must make a lot of money.

5. I must use the creativity, sales, marketing, and finance skills I've honed over the course of my career.

Create Your Timeline

We pick up nuggets of skills and understanding everywhere we go. Take a moment to recognize yours here. Be sure to include every job, no matter how much you disliked it, how menial it may have been, or how unimportant it appears to your life now.

JOB	LIKES	DISLIKES	SKILLS ACQUIRED

CONCLUSION: What have you learned from your work chart? What qualities must you find in every job? Make a list of your non-negotiables.

THE COMMON THREADS

As a producer and creator of television shows, I use all the skills I picked up along the way. I need the math skills I mastered running the TV station, the storytelling skills I picked up in the documentary world, and the ability to access and organize information that I developed at *Seventeen.* What about the skills I learned on the job as a fifteen-year-old? I sell television shows to networks for a living—I'm still a salesgirl above all.

Often, when the Swans who tell me they have *no idea where they're going* perform this exercise, ding dong! they discover they were headed somewhere all along. The Swan Belinda, for example, has spent her life working in different kinds of nursing jobs in hospices. She enjoys her work but couldn't shake the feeling that there is something else out there for her. When she did the timeline exercise, she was stunned to discover that she'd acquired just about all the skills a doctor requires to practice. She just didn't have the degree. What she realized was not where she was going next, but something even more fundamental: Skills and brains were not the things holding her back. Belinda has some work to do to figure out why she never attempted medical school. Now, at least, she is asking the right questions.

Find Your Threads

Take another look at your skill sets in your chart to identify your threads. What do all of your jobs have in common? Which skills have you been able to transfer to other jobs? Can you think of any other positions for which these skills might be useful? Keep in mind that answering this question with a "yes" does not mean you should go get the job. It means you have options. And having options is the key to changing your life.

This Week's Lesson

Drawing up a timeline of your work trajectory helps you keep perspective no matter what job you currently hold. You have a tremendous arsenal of skills, and when you sit down to think about them in such specific terms, you realize that you *do* know where you are going. Being mindful of everything you've done (something made a lot easier with a handy list) will guide you along your way.

Swan Secret: Being mindful of the skills you've picked up along the way makes you a stronger, better worker—no matter what you're doing.

> "Nothing endures but change."
> —HERACLITUS

Vocation

What Is the Key to Your True Happiness?

"What am I going to do with my life?"

I don't think there's a person alive who hasn't uttered these words. Rich or poor, employed or sipping mochas full-time, we're all mindful of having only so many years on earth. Before too long, we want to find meaning and fulfillment in what we do. Above all, we want happiness. The question is: *How do we find it?*

Contentment is easy enough to come by on a summer afternoon with some old friends and a pitcher of piña coladas, but what does it mean to be truly happy? To wake up every morning excited about life? To feel that you are in sync with the universe and doing what you were meant to do?

As a society we've embraced the notion that this kind of fulfillment comes to us if and when we attain beauty, fame, love, and money. But do these things truly fulfill us or do they provide highs that make our lives feel full for an instant and then empty just as quickly?

Since biblical times, a *vocation* has been associated with a spiritual journey, with the imperative to connect one's soul with one's life—to do something more than toil for cash. Being called to your vocation was once synonymous with reporting to the nearest monastery. Today it means going out in the world to do the thing you were meant to do. Obviously the old vocation was simpler in a lot of ways: One call, one location. Now, the options are limitless, and the callings are harder to hear through all the static.

Before they begin considering what to do with their lives, the Swans must define *happiness*. As ugly ducklings who have long felt tormented by the world, many of these young women arrive believing that a physical transformation will finally usher all the pieces of their lives into place, that their new svelte shapes or perky noses will furnish them with the delights life has so far failed to offer. That's a tall order, of course, and any Swan working her way through the grueling three-month program comes to realize that beauty does not guarantee her anything more than ogling passersby, that even after surgery and physical training, she must wake up to the same issues that have concerned her all her life. While getting herself into better physical shape will undoubtedly help, every Swan must learn how to best use her new options to find happiness.

Happiness Is . . .

Before you can feel true happiness, you must know what it is. Don't censor yourself; if you think a nose job or a hunky boyfriend will provide you with fulfillment, write it down. There will be more time to examine your beliefs later.

Define happiness. _____

What would make you truly happy? Why?_____

_____

What would make you look forward to getting up every morning? _____

_____

If your answer to #2 was the same as for #1, give yourself one point. _____

_____

Identify five things (e.g., autumn sunshine, your husband's ears, bodysurfing, etc.) that make you happy: _____

_____

Identify five hobbies/jobs/services that you would be willing to do without being paid for them. Then, explain what is so compelling about this activity that you would do it for free.

1. _____ Why? _____

2. _____ Why? _____

3. _____ Why? _____

4. _____ Why? _____

5. _____ Why? _____

Appreciate the Things That Make Your Life Unique

When I got pregnant, I hit a wall in my personal life and in my career. Privately, I was experiencing a very female mid-life crisis. Yet, at work I was supposed to go on making edgy shows for young Hispanics from immigrant families. Though I had always thrived making such shows, I now found myself in a mismatch. My work wasn't reflecting my new perspective. I had lost my inspiration; I even considered leaving television. And then it hit me: I needed to take my experience and incorporate it into my work. I needed to do something with my new insights—I was no longer the girl whose perspective focused just on young American Latinos. I was becoming someone new, a single mother struggling to stay on course. Why not make a show about women hitting a wall?

Ding dong.

My work was back in sync with my life, and my new project—*The Swan*—was a huge success. Now, I love going to work because I relate to what I'm doing. My professional survival depended upon using my new perspective, and doing so helped me transform my personal crisis into something productive, something with the power to make me happy to wake up in the morning.

You can do the same with the challenges you face. I don't mean you should make a television show about them, but if you find a way to incorporate your unique life experiences into your work—whether it is the job you're paid for, the poetry you write, or the community service you engage in—you will feel fulfilled. Too often, we brush painful experiences under the rug and put on a happy façade for the world. But, it's the challenges we face—not the lazy days by the pool—that make us who we are and give us something special to say to the world. Turn your difficult experiences into ammunition. Learn from them. They're in your life for a reason.

Brainstorm

Discuss one thing you have experienced in the last year that has provided you with a unique perspective: _____

_____

_____

_____

USE YOUR PAST TO MOVE FORWARD

Ever since she could speak, the Swan Merline served as an interpreter for her deaf parents. Throughout her life, she resented her mother and father for their dependency on her, blaming them for her decision not to pursue her interest in psychology. In fact, she came to see the special skills she acquired as a burden. When she arrived on *The Swan,* Merline couldn't shake the feeling that there was something else out there for her, a vocation she might actually choose for herself.

Merline was ignoring her unique voice.

I don't mean to suggest that Merline's parents were right in their reliance upon their daughter—but that fact is now a moot point. This was Merline's childhood; these were the challenges she faced. While there is a lot she can do to improve her life from here, there isn't a whole lot she can do to *create* a new perspective out of thin air. She can add to the voice she has; she can better inform it. She can strengthen it. But she is who she is. The trick is accepting that and using it to find her vocation.

With some therapy, Merline was able to let go of her resentment and focus on the special insights her life afforded her. Though she has

Pop Quiz

What makes you unique?
Write something off the top of your head:

_____

_____

_____

always been aware of her invaluable skills as a language translator, she also came to see some other gifts she'd overlooked: She is in the unique position of living with one foot in two different worlds, possessing the ability to communicate and translate cultural differences between them. As she continued to ponder her situation and the obstacles she faced, she also realized the unique challenges and burdens of growing up with deaf parents. She now knows how to navigate these waters. Perhaps she could develop her untapped interest in psychology and do something to help children just like her.

> "The most important motive for work in school and in life is pleasure in work: pleasure in its result and the knowledge of the value of the result to the community."
>
> —ALBERT EINSTEIN

What Makes You Unique?

In a writing workshop hosted by Sandra Cisneros, I learned that identifying your calling is a matter of thinking about the qualities that make you special in the world. Don't begin with who you want to be, but with who you are.

The categories below are just examples to get your memory working. Dig through any place in your past that had an impact on you. Consider your unique qualities in each area.

What experiences or challenges have given you a unique voice in the workplace?

_____

Your family/home:_____

_____

At school:_____

_____

Activities (sports/church groups/etc.):_____

_____

Health:_____

_____

Other:_____

_____

Turn Tragedy into Transformation

Destiny is the belief that every occurrence in life was meant to happen. The idea is that our experiences are our teachers. Therefore, if we don't learn anything, if we don't use the knowledge we gain from that which happens to us, we've wasted our time. Now, I realize that you may not believe in destiny. In fact, you may believe that life is a series of random events with no meaning. Even if this is the case, I urge you—for the duration of your journey as a Swan—to *suspend disbelief.* Allow yourself to deem all your experiences as your teachers, and to believe that everything has happened to you for a reason, even the tragedies. Not because you deserved it, but because you are the best person to offer this unique insight to the world.

Take Heather Mills McCartney. We all know her as a tall, pretty blonde married to a former Beatle. You may also know that Heather, who lost her leg in an accident in London, is an advocate for land mine removal and the conservation and reuse of discarded prosthetic limbs. In 1998, she was nominated for a Nobel Peace Prize for her assistance in poor, war-torn areas.

Heather has said: "I definitely lost my leg for a reason, without a doubt. Now people are walking who wouldn't be walking if I had not lost my leg." Though I don't know her personally, I would say that Heather Mills McCartney has found her vocation. Did this mission in life just fall from the sky? Of course not. Heather used the knowledge gained from the tragedies in her life to give something unique to the world.

> "The leaders I've met, whatever walk of life they were from, whatever institutions they were presiding over, always referred back to the same failure, something happened to them that was personally difficult, even traumatic, something that made them feel that desperate sense of hitting bottom—as something they thought was almost a necessity. It's as if at that moment the iron entered their soul; that moment created the resilience that leaders need."
>
> —WARREN G. BENNIS, LEADERSHIP EXPERT

Target Your Tragedies

It's hard work finding your calling—you're going to have to return to some of those dark places you thought you would leave behind when you became a Swan. However, if you do not incorporate the tragedies of your life into your vocation, you will find yourself feeling out of sync with the world.

What have you lived through that's given you a unique perspective or unique skills?

Event: _____

Perspective: _____

Skills: _____

Discuss: _____

The Future Is Bright

Now that we've spent time unearthing the challenges in our pasts, it's time for a look at the future—another crucial element in discovering your vocation. Merline, for example, doesn't feel comfortable with her work as an interpreter because there are still so many things she simply hasn't tried yet. She's interested in psychology and photography. She loves to decorate. Though Merline knows one thing—that she has a unique gift in her translator's skills—she will have to explore these other areas before she feels ready for and confident in her vocation.

"You must go after your wish. As soon as you start to pursue a dream, your life wakes up and everything has meaning."

—BARBARA SHER,
MOTIVATIONAL SPEAKER

What do you need to try before you can feel confident in yours?

"The proper function of man is to live, not to exist. I shall not waste my days in trying to prolong them. I shall use my time."

—JACK LONDON

Brainstorm

List five things you would like to try if you had all the time and money in the world.

1. _____ Why? _____

2. _____ Why? _____

3. _____ Why? _____

4. _____ Why? _____

5. _____ Why? _____

This Week's Lesson

Viewing everything that has happened in your life—good and bad—as a source of learning will enable you to not only improve your mood, but also to see your experiences objectively, allowing you to discern lessons at every juncture. Your voice is unique to your own, messy, challenging, wonderful life. By becoming mindful of it, you can share its infinite potential with the world.

Swan Secret: You will find your vocation if you learn to ask yourself the right questions.

Love

Who Loves and Cares for You?

Do you know how to receive? A preliminary self-exam.

Are you a do-it-yourself kind of woman? Or do you let people help you?

1. When you go out on a date with someone (or when you were first dating your boyfriend or spouse), do you allow him to buy dinner, or do you reach for your purse and attempt to divide the check equally? _____

2. If you are walking out to the car carrying a heavy bag and someone you know offers to help, do you let him/her? _____

3. How often do you allow the man in your life to do something for you (i.e., cook dinner, make travel arrangements for you, or pick up your laundry)?

    ☐ Whenever he offers

    ☐ Occasionally

    ☐ Rarely

    ☐ Never

Break Away from Do-It-Yourself Syndrome

Five years ago, I was three notches away from being a full-blown guy. I was the president of a network, I managed huge teams of people, I hired, I fired, I took no prisoners. I was totally independent. And I was miserable.

I don't want to sound ungrateful—I'm indebted to the feminists who got us the vote and better representation in the workplace, to the women who fought hard to give us *options*. The problem is that we later generations of women have found ourselves locked into a new system. The system of *I can do it all without anyone's help.* We can make the money. We can pay the bills. We can make dinner. We can raise the kids. We can do it all. I'm just not clear why we want to. The women I know who do everything, who make the most money and give the most of themselves, are also the least happy. Why? Because they cannot allow other people to *give* to them. Women of our generation were taught to prove their competency, but they were not taught that being cared for could coexist with being strong and independent.

There is a fundamental difference between men's and women's ambitions. Above all things, men want to conquer while women want to love and be loved. The problem is, in order to be loved, we must allow ourselves to be taken care of. Do you remember what it was like to be loved as a child? To accept adoration and care as it came? How is it that we grew up to insist on splitting checks and bills, and *doing it all*? How did we reach the point where we woke up and realized that no one has *given* to us in our whole adult lives? This sensation I speak of is feeling *unloved.*

When you work twelve-hour days in jobs where you behave exactly like a man, how do you go home and turn back into a woman?

Are *you* being cared for?

We all want love. We all want to be cherished. The first step in achieving this is figuring out *who loves you* and how well the love is working.

1. How does your husband/boyfriend or ex show you that he loves you?

   _____

2. How is he different from or similar to the man you imagined yourself ending up with? _____

3. Does he try to give to you? How? _____

_____

4. Does he make you feel cherished?_____

_____

Love Begins at Work

I know how strange that sounds. Doesn't everything "begin at home"? Not when we spend most of our time on the job, reinforcing behavior we take into the rest of our lives. For example, if you are the boss on the job, you begin to think and speak in a certain way because you're results-oriented. Each day you go into work, you reinforce this behavior and, whether you notice or not, you take it home with you, too. Sooner or later, people at work and at home stop coming to you because they think you're all knowing and all powerful—that you don't need them.

Now, women don't consciously choose to relinquish their roles as women, but circumstances often take over and conspire to make us masculine. I'm not saying women shouldn't achieve, or that they shouldn't hold ambitious jobs and want to make lots of money. But, if you're truly interested in being happy, you need to consider where you will be in ten to twenty years. Will you really be fulfilled when you are the CEO? Or, are you climbing that ladder for your ego?

I thought my dream was to run a TV network, but when I got there I realized it was a mismatch for my personality. I'm still very driven to achieve, but now I do it in a different way. Where I once hired people *I had maternal feelings for*, I now hire employees who are *more competent than I*. As a result, I have had to surrender to the people around me, which has afforded me the space and time to enjoy the creative dimension of my work and pass on happy things to the world. By freeing myself from the masculine role of watchdog, I have allowed myself to be more girly, more myself, in my career.

"Where love rules, there is no will to power; and where power predominates, there love is lacking. The one is the shadow of the other."

—CARL JUNG

Work Study

1. What do you do for a living? _____

2. Have you had to take on masculine characteristics in your work?_____

   Describe: _____

3. Are you able to leave your work attitude at work or does it come home with you?

   _____

4. Are you happy at work?_____ Why or why not? _____

   _____

5. What would need to change for you to be happier?_____

   _____

Get Care to Give Care

Whether you're in a relationship now or not, it's important to take a close look at the (last) man in your life to evaluate your current circumstances. Tony Robbins teaches that if you work and behave like a man, you will attract feminine energy—that of someone who needs to be taken care of. Based on what I've seen in my life, he is absolutely right.

But some women like to take care of men, don't they?

No. There is a difference between showing someone love with a backrub and bringing home all the bacon in the household. Even the most powerful women I know, the women who spend twelve-hour days at a rigorous job, *still* want masculine men in their lives. Why? Because they're women. It doesn't matter that most of us cannot actually stand to be taken care of—we all dream of the strong, competent male who will whisk us away from our troubles. So when we end up with feminine guys who need to be taken care of, who allow us, time and again, to take care of everything ourselves, we wind up resenting the hell out of them.

Take Beth Lay. Beth arrived on *The Swan* concerned that her husband might be cheating on her. Beth was bringing in all the money while her husband didn't know what he wanted to do with his life. Although the disparity bothered her, she nonetheless pulled the *don't worry, I can do everything myself* routine, working crazy hours and driving herself into the ground. She took on all the responsibilities in the household: She paid the bills, she cooked, she cleaned.

And he sat on the couch. When Beth's husband became attracted to another woman, she was outraged. How could he? She was working her tail off for him, wasn't she?

I asked Beth whether she took any blame for what had happened. "Why did you allow him to not work?" I asked. "Why did you tell him it was okay to do nothing and then resent him for it?" She admitted she never considered doing things any other way.

I'm not suggesting that you shouldn't do what you want to do for yourself, that you shouldn't work hard and make a lot of money. But don't let someone off the hook just because he does not take responsibility for his (in)actions.

I pushed Beth harder: "If you really believe your husband isn't competent, why are you with him?"

Beth looked stricken. She was still annoyed with her husband, but she was protective enough to make me believe she still loved him.

I made a suggestion: "Take a leap of faith that he's going to be competent and let him be. If he doesn't rise to the occasion, call it a day."

'Fess Up

1. Does your husband/boyfriend/ex do something that you feel he should not be doing? _____

2. Are you harboring resentment for something you condoned in your husband/boyfriend/ex? _____ Explain: _____

3. Can you see how your behavior played any role in the problem? _____

   If *yes*, how? _____

   If *no*, explain: _____

"The tragedy of love is indifference."

—WILLIAM SOMERSET MAUGHAM

CAN YOUR RELATIONSHIP BE SAVED?

The Swans have found that their new attitudes about love have inspired changes in the men in their lives. Although many of the women appeared to be in troubled relationships when they arrived on *The Swan,* nearly all are trying to work things out. The Swans realized two things: 1) they are as responsible as their partners for what happens in their relationships and 2) the men in their lives want women to receive assistance and love, to be womanly, and they in turn want to be pushed, supported, and cherished as men.

The Week's Lesson

In love, women must be women and men must be men. As women, we must be able to receive love and attention; we must stop ourselves from taking on all the responsibility. Above all, we must acknowledge that we need someone else in our lives.

Swan Secret: You will find love if you allow yourself to receive it.

Education

What Are You Learning in the World?

Before reading on, take a moment to list four things you have learned recently:

1. _____

2. _____

3. _____

4. _____

> "The actuality of thought is life."
>
> —ARISTOTLE

Stimulation Is the Key to Happiness

The thing no one ever mentions in self-help books is that one part of not being happy is not learning. By this, I don't mean that if you're feeling down you're not doing anything in the way of introspection—I mean you're probably not doing much else. When we get depressed, our natural inclination is to go inward, even though it's going outward that provides the cure.

When I broke up with my son's father, I pumped myself with information. I read books and magazines, I surfed the web, I went to museums, I walked around my neighborhood and studied every single building with an intensity I once reserved for self-pity—I stimulated myself back to life.

Now, this stimulation is my morning cup of coffee and my afternoon pick-me-up. Whenever I hit a lull, I go out and learn something. It doesn't take much time. It's about altering your mindset.

When the Swans arrive on the show, I ask them what they are learning. Sadly, most of them don't know how to answer. These girls aren't taking in any information, and they're not alone. Learning is something our society places a premium on for the first twenty odd years of our lives and then, boom, it's assumed we know enough to live out the rest of our days. But we can never know enough; there are always more wonderful things to see and read and do out there.

Our world is rich in stimuli. In fact, there is so much information out there that sometimes it is overwhelming. For a lot of us, the natural response is to shut down. As a Swan, you need to turn yourself back on, to load yourself up with as much knowledge as possible because it will:

1. inspire you;

2. serve as a natural anti-depressant;

3. put you into a state of gratitude in the world;

4. facilitate your transformation.

Education takes you out of yourself, your problems, and your past. It transports you into an active dreamland, a world of infinite ideas and possibilities. Do these exercises and you will find yourself overflowing with ideas and inspiration to keep you going through the day. Once you begin to take in what's out there, once you feed yourself daily eye and brain candy, you'll find that you can't stay upset for very long. Swan's Honor.

Intellectual Stim

There's so much to learn in the world that will make you feel good about life and, above all, give you ideas. By reading books and magazines, browsing websites and doing other activities that were created to further our store of knowledge, we engage the wordy, logical left hemisphere of our brains. This exercise isn't about mastering a subject; intellectual stim is concerned with fun and inspiration—engage in these activities only insofar as they inspire you.

TOOLS: A journal, a pair of scissors, and either a couple of baskets or large bins able to fit roughly ten magazines worth of loose paper. I keep twelve colored bins—which I found on a decorating site for children's rooms—in my office, broken into categories like: *house, personal, to buy, to read,* and *The Swan*.

OBJECTIVE: Clip and save *anything* that strikes your fancy. Yes, anything. I don't care if it's a picture of an ant-farm or a single word with a nice sound. If it interests you, clip it, print it out, or jot it down in your notebook.

GOAL: Though you should begin with a weekly stim assignment, quickly attempt to work learning into your everyday—and *always* write down or clip ideas that are compelling. Each day, go through one bin, throwing out clips that no longer speak to you and replacing the ones that do in the bin—this exercise should take about fifteen minutes and will sufficiently inspire your day.

ORGANIZATION: Intellectual stim is meant to inspire you, so storing your clips in filing cabinets won't do any good—you'll never look at them again. When you're finished browsing and clipping, organize your ideas into categories and place them into your baskets or bins accordingly. To make your learning fun and inviting, use colored or decorated bins without tops. The piles should not exceed the limit of the bin—you don't want to overwhelm yourself. It's important to keep things orderly so that you can access your ideas whenever you like. To this end, make a routine of going through your bins—the more frequently you do it, the more manageable the piles and also the steadier your inspiration. Do your best to keep the things that inspire you close at hand; put special books on the coffee table, photos on the wall, sayings on your computer's desktop, etc.

> "Knowledge must come through action."
>
> —SOPHOCLES

What Your Stim Is Stimulating

This chapter's exercises engage your cerebrum—the part of your brain that holds your memories, allows you to plan, and enables you to imagine and think, recognize friends, read books, and play games. The cerebrum is split into two hemispheres, with the ability to form words lying primarily in the left hemisphere (intellectual stim), while the right hemisphere controls many abstract reasoning skills (sensual stim).

IDEAS FOR INTELLECTUAL STIM

MAGAZINE CLIPPING: I'm a word person, so for me, clipping is a daily activity. I read about 170 magazines each month, and I clip anything and everything that interests me, from stories about home decorating to pictures I take a liking to. I have fantasy ideas in my bins (how to run a restaurant), gift ideas (new computer equipment for my son), lists of words I love (just because I like them), etc. I clip anything that gets my mind working and often there's no rhyme or reason to it—at least none that I'm aware of at the time. If it interests me, it goes in my bin.

WEB-SURFING: Now, I'm not one of those people who will gladly spend nine hours surfing the web. As in every area of my life, I find ways to economize my time. Try visiting television show websites—they're an appallingly underused resource, offering everything from booklists to recipes to news. My favorites: The *Today Show* homepage (www.msnbc.com/onair/nbc/today), MarthaStewart.com, and Oprah.com.

BOOKS: I'm a bookaholic, and as I've said, I want to find something I'll enjoy without wasting a lot of time. So, I go to the websites.

If I'm reading, I'll jot down ideas I get in my journal—and of course, any word I like goes in, as well. If I'm reading an art book I find particularly inspiring, I keep it out on my coffee table at home.

Sensual Stim

The other day, I got into my car and someone said, "I love your car," and I thought, *how quickly I take things for granted!* A new car, and after a week it's no big deal. To combat this sort of ennui, I make believe whatever I'm doing is new. I pretend I'm driving in my car for the first time, or when I walk around my neighborhood I imagine I'm on vacation and I've never seen any of the stores or the signs or the houses before.

How many people know every little shop in their community? Who takes the time to ask about a building's history? Who knows all the people who work and live there? Who really takes the time to appreciate the small, wonderful qualities of their own neighborhood? When I do this exercise, I become so engrossed in all the lovely little details of my neighborhood that I can actually become lost. *Look at this little store*, I think, *look at this sign.* I attempt to learn as much as I can about the buildings (When were they built? What was here before?) and the people (Who knew the owner of the deli hasn't left town for a weekend since 1970?). Try this exercise when you're feeling blue and I promise, things will look a lot better in a half an hour.

For a one-hour sensual stim excursion, attend a museum exhibit, see a movie, or listen to new music. (I love going to Sephora to admire and sample all the makeup.) The key to appreciating this form of stimulation is to learn to let yourself enjoy pleasurable stimuli. Write down ideas in your journal—a word, a phrase, a smear of lipstick on a page. Make a record of your moment.

> "We are an intelligent species and the use of our intelligence quite properly gives us pleasure. In this respect, the brain is like a muscle. When it is in use we feel very good. Understanding is joyous."
>
> —CARL SAGAN

What do you do if you don't have time for such things? You multitask. I have a kid and a business. That's why I use the television websites and Tivo the shows I like to watch. Or, if I want to read, I sit my son next to me, give him some comics and coloring books and say, "Here's your pile and here's mine." And then we just sit and read.

Six Degrees of Stimulation

The funny thing about the ideas that inspire you is that there are always six degrees of separation before you get to what you were supposed to learn, before you understand why something captivated you. It's never a direct link, but that's okay, because the thing in between the original and the connection? Inspiration! You know the wonderful quickening sensation in your brain and heart when something inspires you? I love that feeling—and it's more important than most people know.

Besides, allowing your mind to ramble freely and pluck the sights, sounds, and information from the world can help you discover your vocation. Swan Tawnya, for example, spent a lot of time browsing the Internet, saving information about running businesses and dance, among other things. When she looked back at her clippings and notes, it occurred to her that she might want to start a dance studio of her own. We discussed the possibility, but something didn't seem quite right. Tawnya went back to her book and, in rereading it, discovered that she wasn't really an entrepreneur. She didn't enjoy being the visionary—what she loved was the business. Why not look into buying a franchise? Tawnya spent more time exploring her options and buying a franchise is what she's attempting to do now that she's back home. She hopes to be the proud owner of a small business. Who knew those hours of stim could transform her career!

This Week's Lesson

It's amazing where stimulating your mind will take you. Besides improving your mood and making your mind and senses happy with fun stuff to chew on, you're moving toward your goals. It doesn't matter if the course is not immediately clear. Cut out pictures, print articles, and jot down notes, and your world will come into focus a lot faster than you'd ever have believed.

Swan Secret: Learning about the world around you is the key to happiness.

Family and Friends

Are the People Around You Truly Supportive?

Before you begin, make a list of friends and family to whom you are closest.

1. _____

2. _____

3. _____

4. _____

5. _____

6. _____

7. _____

8. _____

9. _____

10. _____

Support System Roll Call

If you asked me to identify my support system, I would list a handful of friends and my parents. If anything in the world happened to my son or me, those two proud Cubans in Miami would be on the first flight out.

There were times when I was growing up that my mother didn't feel very good about herself. To lift her spirits, my father would jokingly say to me in his booming, Cuban accent: "Nely, you're the smartest girl in the world, but you're not as pretty as your mother was when she was young." Although I understood he said these things to make my mother feel good about her looks, his words still really hurt because being beautiful in a Latino family is a big deal.

When I look back on my life, it astounds me how much power my father's lighthearted comment had over me. To this day, I can be in a meeting, and no matter who else is in the room, I believe I am the smartest person in attendance. But for most of my life, I also never felt beautiful, no matter what efforts I put toward my appearance. Of course, it isn't as if my father called before each meeting to say, "Now Nely, remember, you're the smartest but you're not the prettiest." On the contrary: I heard these words so many times over the course of my life that I rerecorded them in my own, harsher voice. My father didn't have to say a word; I had become my own critic.

In therapy, I discovered why these words were so destructive: I was replaying the scene in my head through the eyes of the eight-year-old I was when I first heard them. When I attempted to re-experience them again as an adult, I heard the silliness in my father's comment as well as my mother's pain. My dad was just trying to remind her how lovely she was. He would never have said anything to hurt me intentionally. Understanding this helped me feel better about myself.

In fact, last year I was just chosen as one of the "25 Most Beautiful People" for *People* magazine's Español issue. Have my looks changed that substantially? No, but my attitude has. After years of feeling ugly, I decided I was going to feel beautiful. It was that simple. I put it out into the world that I feel good about myself and people have responded accordingly.

The Broken Record

The criticism you receive from your family and friends becomes what I call your *broken record,* and most women I know hear its music at the most inopportune times. Have a big meeting? As soon as you enter, the brain boom box hits play: *You really must have pulled a fast one to get to this position!* Getting your hair highlighted? The song starts up again, laughing at you: *Ha. Are you trying to be pretty now?*

The broken record is no fun . . . until you figure out who made the original and delete the track from your head.

Who Wrote the Songs?

Go back over your previous list and identify those members who, though they love you and you love them, have helped generate your broken record. Next, either state the exact words or phrases they use or write down the gist, making sure to identify the area of your life that was criticized.

1. Name:_____ Recording/s:_____ Area: _____

2. Name:_____ Recording/s:_____ Area: _____

3. Name:_____ Recording/s:_____ Area: _____

4. Name:_____ Recording/s:_____ Area: _____

5. Name:_____ Recording/s:_____ Area: _____

6. Name:_____ Recording/s:_____ Area: _____

7. Name:_____ Recording/s:_____ Area: _____

8. Name:_____ Recording/s:_____ Area: _____

9. Name:_____ Recording/s:_____ Area: _____

10. Name:_____ Recording/s:_____ Area: _____

SMASHING THE BROKEN RECORD

A couple years ago, I took my new boyfriend home to meet my parents. When I introduced him to my mother, she shook his hand and said, "Oh well, I hope you can deal with her. She's very difficult." We went on with the evening, to dinner and more conversations, but this comment sat with me all night. I felt awful. In fact, it took me a full twenty-four hours to process what had happened. To sort things out, I drew up a list of as many incidents like this that I could remember. It was disturbingly long. It was really painful for me to realize my mother had done this sort of thing to me with every man I'd ever dated, either by warning the man himself or making it clear to me that she believed I would screw things up.

The next step I took was to consider why my mother had said these hurtful things. What was in it for her to have these men believe something negative about me? For me to be a failure in love? I asked myself a million questions about my mother, and then I remembered my father's words from my childhood: "You're the smartest, but you aren't the prettiest." I realized that my mother must have experienced many disappointments in life, but love and beauty were her treasured successes. She was the pretty one; that's why I had to be the smart one.

So I called her up and said, "Mom, I don't believe that you would really want a man to think badly of your daughter; I think someone must have really hurt you and really criticized you in your life for you to do that to me."

Now keep in mind that I was speaking to a woman who had been having the same conversation with my boyfriends all my life. And yet, when I forced her to examine her words, she heard them as if for the first time. And she was distressed by what she heard, by her behavior, and by the knowledge that she had hurt me for so many years.

After that, I could see my mother for who she really was: a woman who is as flawed as every other human being out there. Most important, the hurtful things she said weren't about

Filter Fodder

Here are some basic questions you can ask yourself whenever a conversation gives you a weird feeling and you need to get to the bottom of it.

What would make _____ want to say that to me?

What's in it for _____ if I don't grow in this area?

What is _____'s history in this area that might be relevant to his/her discomfort with me?

me, but really about her. This was an opportunity to review all the messages she and my father had given me over the years, and you know what? I realized that I'm not as smart as I think, but I'm a lot prettier than I used to be!

It's time, once and for all, to take a hammer to *your* broken record.

Break the Record

Write down the names of people from the previous list who have helped generate your broken record, and consider what you know about their lives. Think along the following lines: Why might they be uncomfortable with your ability to grow in this area? What have they left undone in their own lives?

1. Name:_____ Criticism: _____

   Possible reasons for his/her discomfort in this area: _____

2. Name:_____ Criticism: _____

   Possible reasons for his/her discomfort in this area: _____

3. Name:_____ Criticism: _____

   Possible reasons for his/her discomfort in this area: _____

4. Name:_____ Criticism: _____

   Possible reasons for his/her discomfort in this area: _____

5. Name:_____ Criticism: _____

   Possible reasons for his/her discomfort in this area: _____

Develop Your Filter

You know that sensation in the pit of your stomach when someone says something critical? That feeling might erupt on the spot, or take hours or days to kick in. The time span doesn't matter; if you have that feeling, you need to run the comment that spawned it through your *filter*.

When *The Swan* first began airing, for example, I was talking to an old friend on the phone. She mentioned that she'd seen me on television, and added in a sarcastic tone, "So you want to be on TV now, too?"

When I hung up the phone, I felt really weird. This friend wasn't being supportive, and I needed to know why. She was either concerned about my goal, or she had a problem of her own. I went through a list of questions that I've come to call my *filter*. *Why would a friend say something hurtful to me? What was in it for her to make me feel self-conscious about appearing on a television show?* And then the answer popped into my mind: A long time ago, we had a conversation in which she mentioned that her dream was to be an anchorwoman. Well, my friend had never realized this dream. This comment, I understood, was about her. Although it stung to hear my friend say something so mean-spirited, I realized that her comment had nothing to do with me. And so I let it pass.

APPLYING YOUR FILTER TO THE WORLD

Equipped with your new filter, you can decide what information comes in and what stays out. The thing is, even with the most hurtful criticisms taken care of, there are still those day-to-day comments that can ruin an afternoon, or did before you constructed a filter. Consider the saleswoman who looks at you when you enter the boutique and says, "All the extra-larges are in the basement." Or, the traffic cop who laughs in your face as he hands you a ticket. Or maybe the facialist who turns the light on over your face and tells you your skin is abominable. My initial reaction is to scream, "What's your problem?!" But then I run it through the filter: Is this really about me? Does this person really care one way or another about me? *No.* You see, the filter has another use: It puts you back in your place.

I keep my imaginary shield up all the time. Those nasty little comments at the salon may not be as important to me as my relationship with my mother, but why not let them hit the shield and fall flat on the ground anyway? Take in only the information that helps you grow, and leave the destructive stuff to the birds.

This Week's Lesson

The criticism you receive from your family and friends becomes your broken record, playing disapproving music whenever you set out to make a change or try something new or bold. Luckily, developing your filter will enable you to keep this negative energy at bay. Armed with your filter, *you* decide what information comes in and what stays out.

Swan Secret: Use your filter wisely, and you'll see the best in all of your friends—and they'll see the best in you.

Forgiveness

Do You Hold on to the Things That Have Hurt You?

Have you ever been at a party, happily chatting away, when suddenly someone enters the room and fills you with a desperate urge to run and hide?

We all have people in our lives that inspire such terror: an ex-boyfriend with whom you weren't totally fair, an old friend who betrayed you, or a coworker with whom you never hit it off. Whoever that emotional terrorist happens to be, that desire to flee is telling you one thing: You are ripe for forgiveness.

In our culture, we often say, "I regret what I haven't done." That's a valid emotion; in fact, I've written this book to encourage you to take the bull by its horns, as they say, and minimize the chances of such regret. But part of feeling comfortable in your own skin is evaluating the things you have done . . . *all* the things, including the bad. Most of us are only too happy to forget painful incidents; but if we ignore them they sit like cancers on our conscience, and they affect our efforts at forward movement.

Don't be afraid to face those demons. I know from experience that forgiveness can release some of the sweetest energy in the universe. And it's so simple we seem to forget its power. The other day, for example, one of my employees was extremely irritable during a meeting and said some inappropriate things to a colleague. He raised his voice. He snapped at someone. I was a little surprised by his behavior and, when I saw him a couple hours later, he was remorseful.

"I was really out of line this morning," he said. "I'm sorry." Then, he asked me if I could forgive him. Now, I don't know if anyone has ever asked forgiveness of you, but when it happens, you have no choice but to let it go. In an instant, the negative energy is gone.

I've found that one of the hardest things in life is finding out who you truly are, for better and for worse. Not so you can relish it, but so that you can learn from it, clear it off your conscience, and move on. The process of forgiveness is a little like looking at an X-ray of your soul. You hold your whole life up to the light and look for the scars, the fissures, and the pain, and then you try to make them better. It's simple. Just try it.

> "No one makes you feel inferior without your consent."
>
> —ELEANOR ROOSEVELT

Who Are Your Emotional Terrorists?

Who hurt you and left a scar that hasn't quite healed? List all those people who would inspire you to run and hide if you spotted them at Starbucks:

1. _____

2. _____

3. _____

4. _____

5. _____

6. _____

7. _____

8. _____

9. _____

10. _____

Learning to Forgive

Now that you've developed your filter (see Week 5: Family and Friends), you'll find a thousand different uses for it, beginning with forgiving those who have hurt you.

I used my filter a few years ago when a good girlfriend and I had a falling out. She was a wonderful woman, but she was constantly getting herself into messes, and I was in turn bailing her out. I realized that I had become codependent, that I was in effect helping her behave irresponsibly, and that I would have to cut her off, for her well-being and mine. A year later, I found she was trashing me in every conceivable way. I was hurt and angry, and my first thought was to get back at her. After cooling off, I realized that if I didn't find a way to forgive her, I would only be poisoning myself. So I put her actions through my filter:

What kind of a person would do this to someone she had once called her friend?

My answer came swiftly: *A person with nothing to lose.*

I wrote more questions: *How could she do this to me? What did I do to deserve this?*

Answer: *I allowed it to happen by not creating appropriate boundaries.*

My subconscious was right. My old friend was not in a good place. As I continued writing my filter questions, I considered her career and her personal life, and the many obstacles she'd faced in the last few years. As soon as I understood her difficulties, my pain and rage gave way to pity. I felt sorry for her, and that made it surprisingly easy to forgive her. I couldn't help her, and she wasn't asking for my help; it was easy to move on. I didn't give her, or her letter, another thought.

Using your filter will allow you to be more compassionate, to be mindful of another's experience. You'll quickly realize that people seldom act out of sheer malice, but are propelled by something deep inside themselves, something they're probably not even aware of. This isn't about condoning bad behavior, but about *understanding* it.

"Who, then, can so softly bind up the wound of another as he who has felt the same wound himself?"

—THOMAS JEFFERSON

Filter-a-terrorist

Choose one terrorist from your previous list. Write down what he or she did to hurt you, and run those actions through your filter by attempting to explain why. Write as much as you want for as long as you like. Buy a lined legal pad; fill all the pages if you have to. Forgiveness often takes time, but I'm living proof that it works.

Name: _____ Action: _____

_____

Filter Questions:

1. What kind of a person would do this to me? Someone evil? Vindictive? Jealous?

   _____

2. What is going on in this person's life to make him or her do this?

   _____

3. How am I going to respond to this person?_____

   _____

4. Does this person have any real power over me?_____

   _____

5. Is the person he/she thinks he/she sees the same person I am? How are the two different?_____

   _____

6. Do not allow yourself to be a victim. What is your culpability in the situation?

   _____

Diagnosing Yourself as a Terrorist

Forgiveness isn't a one-way street. No matter how sweet and kind you think you are (and I know I think I'm pretty sweet and kind!), there are people out there who will want to run and hide when they see you at a party. In fact, when I wrote up my list of victims, I realized that I had terrorized eleven people, and that I myself had been victimized by only five terrorists. Was it really possible that I was more of a terrorist than a victim? It was painful to face this, and my instinct was to put a movie on and forget I'd ever even broached the subject of my own terrorism. I mean, really! Could I be such a bad person? But then I decided to face it. I had made my share of mistakes. But brushing reality under the rug wasn't going to make it go away, and I'd learn nothing from it. Until I developed the courage to face up to my mistakes, I'd keep making them over and over.

When I was twenty-three, for example, I briefly dated a man who was getting a divorce, but was officially still married. We broke off the relationship when my mother convinced me to do the right thing. "I did not raise you to do these things," she said. "You need to make it right." This lover and I moved on with our lives. But ten years later, when I sat down to consider whom I might have hurt, I thought not of him, but of his kids. I had a child of my own now. I often see the world through his eyes. I was looking back with an entirely new perspective. *Was I still at fault?*

Yes, went the heavily accented voice in my ears.

My mother has been wrong about a lot of things, but I'm grateful for her tough love. We all need people in our lives who are not afraid to intercede when we've stepped off our paths.

Sure enough, one day a friend called to tell me that a young woman had gone to his office to interview for an internship. She was trying to break into television. When my friend told her to call me, not knowing that we had a little history together, the young woman's eyes teared up. "I can't. It would bring back too many bad memories."

I felt awful. This young woman was eleven when I had that brief dalliance with her father, and she had been pained to know that he loved someone else. Was this my fault? Well, we could argue that point at length, but it's moot; the real point is that I felt I needed to make amends. So I called her. That conversation turned out to be one of the most difficult and emotional conversations in my life. Many years had passed, but this young woman was still in pain, and I was finally taking responsibility for my part in it. I asked for her to forgive me, and she did. It gave us both the closure we'd been seeking.

In the course of that call, I also discovered something unexpected: When you ask someone for forgiveness, it makes it easier for you to forgive others. The woman I am today, at forty, would never date a married man, whether or not he said he was getting a divorce. But I was a different girl at twenty-three, a girl who saw nothing wrong with that scenario. Alas, naïveté is no excuse. We must all take responsibility for every stage

> "If you give to a thief he cannot steal from you, and he is then no longer a thief."
>
> —WILLIAM SAROYAN

of our lives. Revisiting my many incarnations makes it easier for me to understand other people's behavior. Everyone is a work in progress. Everyone goes through periods they are not proud of later. And everyone deserves forgiveness.

IDENTIFY YOUR VICTIMS

Who have you hurt, directly or indirectly? It can be a boyfriend you strung along, a child whose feelings you hurt during elementary school, or a waiter you treated shabbily. Identifying them may seem like quite a task, but subconsciously you know who they are. Ask the questions; the answers will come.

Who would not want to see you at a party?

1. Name:_____ What you did: _____

2. Name:_____ What you did: _____

3. Name:_____ What you did: _____

4. Name:_____ What you did: _____

5. Name:_____ What you did: _____

6. Name:_____ What you did: _____

7. Name:_____ What you did: _____

8. Name:_____ What you did: _____

9. Name:_____ What you did: _____

10. Name:_____ What you did: _____

What Now?

My old friend who had trashed me publicly has been trying for months to tell me she is sorry. Unfortunately, she tells everyone I know except me. She needs my forgiveness so that she can have some closure, but she is going about it too indirectly.

Now that you've identified some of your victims, how do you find closure? For best results, you need to make direct contact with these people. You can call them, you can write—it's up to you. It's simple. A phone call. A letter. Flowers. Something truly from the heart. Seek forgiveness, and you shall find it. And, yes, you'll experience some discomfort. But that feeling will pass quickly—I know, I've been there—and when you're done you'll find than an unburdened soul can truly soar.

FORGIVING YOURSELF

Sometimes forgiving others goes hand in hand with forgiving yourself, especially when it comes to family. Take *The Swan* pageant winner Rachel. When Rachel was a little girl, her father told her that he didn't expect much of her. All her life, she was haunted by this comment. No matter what, she couldn't shake the feeling that she was inferior, and was depressed to no end. As a result she didn't have the energy, or the inclination, to take care of herself. But while she was in the program, she found the wherewithal to forgive her father, and soon discovered that she had one more person to forgive: "*Me.* I was just as responsible as my father. I never gave myself a chance to achieve anything."

Your Own Worst Enemy

What have you done to yourself that wasn't fair or loving? How have you kept yourself back? What should you forgive in yourself?

Free yourself of this burden using your filter questions.

Things to forgive yourself for: _____

_____

Filter Questions:

1. What kind of a person would have done this? (consider *who* you were at the time)

   _____

2. What was going on in your life when you did this? _____

   _____

3. Would you do something like this now? Why or why not? (In other words, figure out what you have learned along the way.) _____

_____

This Week's Lesson

Forgiveness is one of the most important tools of transformation. You'll find that when you've accomplished it—even with one person—you are propelled another few feet into your new life. Progress comes with freeing yourself of the past by taking a good, hard look at yourself and those in your life, for better and for worse.

Swan Secret: Forgiveness doesn't take energy, it gives energy.

> "Holding on to anger is like grasping a hot coal with the intent of throwing it at someone else; you are the one getting burned."
>
> —BUDDHA

Spirituality

Where Do You Find Your Faith?

You've Got to Have Faith

A long time ago, my mother said to me, "Nely, the greatest gift in life is learning how to wait for things." Though I didn't realize it then, my mother's comment was all about faith, the faith that what we need in life will materialize; the faith that the situations through which we struggle will work out for the best; the faith that we will be taken care of if we do our work.

I hate waiting. But that just makes me human. Have you ever noticed that all of us want what we want when we want it? I admit it. I get frustrated when I've worked hard for something and I don't get it right away. I cry, I scream, I pound my fists. And then . . . nothing happens.

Sometimes we don't realize that there's a path for us—a path we must wait for. By that I don't mean there's someone out there writing the script of your life; I don't believe that. We're the ones who decide, and we make decisions every day, but the things we learn from those decisions are seldom immediately apparent. The wait can be maddening—especially when you've worked hard to make something happen. Unfortunately, the universe doesn't care—you have a lesson to learn, and you will wait until the cows come home if you have to.

For years, for example, it troubled me that I attracted addictive types of people into my life. It was a constant issue with my friends, the men I dated, and the people I hired. I worked a lot on myself, and I eventually understood my lesson: I can't fix other people; I need to take care of myself and my son and let everyone else take care of his or her own issues. Over the course of a few years, I came to terms with this fact, and I stopped trying to fix other people, and in due course I noticed an amazing thing: I had stopped attracting addictive people into my life. It took many years, and it was a long, frustrating wait, but I learned something else along the way: Once you've learned your lesson, no one can ever take it from you. Sure, you may stumble and fall from time to time, but in your heart you know you can do it, you know you have the tools to move beyond this particular problem.

It's just like my mother said. Patience is a gift. But patience has its limits, too. A person who sits in front of the television hoping for good things to happen doesn't understand the meaning of patience. Patience isn't about inaction. It's about moving forward even when you know that results are seldom instant. Moving forward is the key. You still have to get out of bed in the morning and eat three square meals a day and work and make your way in the world. And while you're doing all of that, do one important thing: Get in touch with yourself. It's time to determine what it is you need and what you have to do to get it. At the end of the day, you'll discover one simple truth: The answers are inside you. All you have to do is access them.

That's what this chapter's all about.

Wish Upon a Star

Name one thing you have been waiting and working for that has yet to materialize.

_____

1. How long have you been waiting? _____

2. What steps have you taken to achieve it:

a. _____

b. _____

c. _____

d. _____

e. _____

Journey Inward

As you progress in your work as a Swan, you will need to *go inward*—both to find peace while you wait and to make your wait shorter. Going inward can mean whatever you want: daily yoga practice, long walks, listening to inspiring music, or weekly church visits, among other things. Your method doesn't have to be trendy or socially acceptable. The key is getting yourself into a zone where you can focus.

I've tried absolutely everything, which is the only way to find the method that works best for you. If you're the type of person who gets bored easily, establish a few different routines. I find, for example, that I can access my zone simply by taking a shower. But, because I like a bit more stimuli sometimes, I also go to church, meditate, and write in my journal. It depends on what I need on any given day.

Though I was raised Catholic, I've never felt particularly connected to religious dogma. I do, however, appreciate the peace of mind I get from the rituals, the music and the readings. Attending church—any church, be it Methodist, Southern Baptist, or Catholic—takes me into my zone. The religion doesn't matter to me. I've found a couple ministers I like, and on Sundays I pick one to listen to and go in and focus on my issues, jotting down notes as they come to me. Sometimes the minister will say something I find interesting and illuminating. Sometimes not. But either way is fine. Being in church is enough to put me into my zone.

If going inward is new to you, try listening to a piece of music. Find a song that touches you, that makes you cry or gives you goose bumps. Listen to a voice that really takes you somewhere. I often try to make music a component in my faith—I attend churches with incredible music, I go to the symphony, I put on Sarah McLachlan while I'm writing in my journal.

THE ISOLATION TECHNIQUE

As with every other area in your life, faith requires that you ask yourself the right questions. Like Ben Franklin (see page 25), I identify one issue for the week, writing it out on a page in my journal and practicing what I call the *isolation technique.*

The isolation technique involves focusing on a single theme each week. It's that simple. Focusing on a single subject saves you from being overwhelmed and adds power to your contemplation, allowing you to consider the issue from every angle and to take in only what is relevant to you. The isolation technique allows you to see the world through the prism of your subject.

Your theme can be anything you want to work out in your life. Some weeks, for example, my issue is not feeling abundance. Now, that could mean anything to you, but to me it means that my life does not feel full enough. It might stem from being lonely or it might mean I'm just plain bored. The first question I write down in my notebook is *How can I feel abundance?* And then, I go into my zone, armed with my issue, and look for answers.

Find Your Faith

Isolate your issue for the week. It may be the same subject you cited in the previous exercise or it might be something specifically relevant to *this* week in your life.

Issue: _____

Now, write out a few questions to ponder while you're in your zone:

1._____

2._____

3._____

The Answers Are All Around You

Something amazing happens when you focus in on your topic: You find relevant information everywhere. Go into your zone, and you'll discover the minister, yoga instructor, or meditation guru is actually addressing a topic relevant to your theme. If you're a walker, you'll see something—a group of people performing, perhaps, or a billboard that provides insight. You'll get the feeling *you were meant to be there.* Insight is everywhere; your antennae just need to be tuned in.

To fine-tune these feelers, you might try to engage in both private and public modes of going inward. Some days, a minister may be too distracting, while at other times you'll find that listening to a story, poem, or insightful sermon commingles nicely with your inner voice. When you make going inward a routine, you'll condition yourself to finding answers. I get excited every Sunday morning, for instance, just thinking that I'm going to hear something relevant to my life, that I'm going to make a connection.

---

1. Schedule an hour or two this week to go inward. It can be public or private; it can be anything you like. Try yoga, meditation, religious services, listening to music, or a long walk.

2. Write out your week's issue and some questions.

3. Once in your zone, remember to jot down notes, ideas, and connections.

Capitalize on Good Times

What should you do when something amazing happens in your life? When you feel great? When the thing you've been working toward for years has finally materialized? Should you be out celebrating? Sure. Do you still need to go inward? *Yes.*

When the Swan Rachel was crowned during the show's final beauty pageant, I experienced a magical moment. Colored flakes fluttered down from the sky, fireworks lit up the stage, and I couldn't take my eyes off the confident beauty who stood before me: she was a woman transformed. I was moved to tears because I was so proud of Rachel and of all of these young women, but I was equally proud of myself. I'd finally created a job that fulfilled my soul. I'd worked hard, and it paid off. I felt immensely grateful.

I celebrated with the girls and the crew, and then I went home to write in my journal.

> "If you can keep your faith and you can learn from your mistakes, I think you can turn anything around."
>
> —SEAN COMBS (P. DIDDY)

My issue that night was *invention*. I had invented the perfect job, and I wanted to record how it unfolded so that I could access that wonderful feeling again—literally. I keep all my diaries together on a bookshelf, dated and labeled as if they were volumes of an encyclopedia. And indeed they are resource material. I go back to these diaries time and time again. Try it for yourself.

That night, with my pen poised over my journal, I asked myself the usual questions: *Why was this experience magical for me? What have I learned from this show? What did I learn from tonight? When have I felt like this before?*

Would you believe that crowning the Swan reminded me of giving birth to my son? I experienced the same exalted sensation of slow motion, the same burst of joyful tears, and the same feeling of watching a new life beginning. I felt nourished by happiness, my own and that of everyone around me.

When something wonderful happens in your life, you need to reach for your journal and write down every scrumptious detail, describing how you got there, what you felt, who was there, and what occurred, minute by scrumptious minute. Yes, it will consume half an hour of your time, but that moment will be enshrined forever, and you may find yourself going back to it, time and again, in the years ahead.

> The next time you experience joy, record the moment in your journal. Don't wait until the next day or the next week—get that information on the page that very day. Consider every detail: the way you feel, the sounds, the sights, the smells around you. Think back to other moments when you felt the same way, and look for the connections. Then put the journal on a shelf for future reference.

This Week's Lesson

Whether it's listening to Mozart or lying on the couch counting the revolutions made by your ceiling fan, going inward to your zone is a crucial part of your transformation process. Answers won't come to you whenever you seek them and results can take years. Faith furnishes you with a focused sense of peace that will nourish you while you wait.

Swan Secret: All of the answers are inside of you.

Fun

What Do You Do for Fun?

I have never been fun. I know what fun is and I know how it feels to have it, but I, personally, am not fun. Perhaps this is why fun is something I covet above all things, why I have always surrounded myself with fun people and worked in fun jobs, why I date fun men, and why I thank God every day that I gave birth to a child with a good, strong sense of fun.

I keep lists of fun things I would never do. I order brochures for vacations I would never take, and I download information about safaris and spa retreats I consider a waste of time and money. Yet I organize and prioritize these ideas in lists such as Big Fun (those things I consider hugely uneconomical and/or time consuming), Fun Dates (amusing things to do in about an hour), Fun with Son, etc. When I'm feeling dreamy or extravagant I pull my journal out of my purse and flip through my lists. Usually, I just reread them, but with some regularity I place a check by one particular activity and go out and do it.

Of course, a lot of women other than me don't know how to have fun. Our lives are too busy, our children too demanding, and our schedules too important for a little free-spirited amusement. What we're overlooking, of course, is that having fun is crucial to our well-being. Fun helps us let off steam that otherwise curdles our insides. Fun keeps us grounded and actually bolsters our immune systems. In addition, studies have shown that people who laugh more tend to take better care of themselves than those who are angry and stressed. If this surprises you, you need to have more fun.

I'll be right there with you.

Fun-o-meter

List everything you've done in the last month that was fun. Then, score the item's fun factor on a scale of 1 to 10. (10 being unbelievably fun and 1 being barely any fun at all.)

1. Fun thing:_____ Fun score:_____

2. Fun thing:_____ Fun score:_____

3. Fun thing:_____ Fun score:_____

4. Fun thing:_____ Fun score:_____

5. Fun thing:_____ Fun score:_____

6. Fun thing:_____ Fun score:_____

7. Fun thing:_____ Fun score:_____

8. Fun thing:_____ Fun score:_____

9. Fun thing:_____ Fun score:_____

10. Fun thing:_____ Fun score:_____

Allow Your Jealousy to Guide You

If I read about a celebrity enjoying an African safari, I am beside myself with envy. "Why do they get to go on a safari? I want to go on a safari!" It doesn't matter that I'm just returning from an island trip listed in my fun file. I get jealous when other people are having fun.

Now, as you know from musing, jealousy comes in very handy when you need some direction in your life. This applies to work and beauty, and it applies just as well to fun. Just the other morning, for example, I developed a stomachache while reading a newsletter from my *Mommy and Me* e-mail group. I saw that another mother asked for our advice in planning a spa weekend. Immediately, I became so perturbed that I had to take a break and leave my computer. I asked myself a series of questions: *Was the group not clicking? Was something upsetting me at work? Was I just in a bad mood that morning?*

No! My mind bellowed. *I want to go on a spa weekend!*

I was jealous—again—that someone else was planning to have fun. Easily solved. I took out my journal and added *Spa Weekend* to my list of fun to-dos and stapled the *Mommy and Me* e-mail with the many suggestions to the back of the page. I felt better immediately.

Coveting Fun

List five fun things other people have done recently that you would like to do. It doesn't matter how frivolous or beyond your means you might think these things are.

1. _____

2. _____

3. _____

4. _____

5. _____

EXCUSES FOR NOT HAVING FUN

(Check those that apply to you.)

☐ MY JOB IS FUN . . .

No, it isn't. Job fun and recreational fun are not the same things. You must make a distinction between these two categories in order to reap all the benefits of fun. I happen to have a very fun job, too. I mean, who gets to go to a beauty pageant and crown a Swan? But, if that's all you're doing for recreation, you're a workaholic. You have to create a fun life outside of work and outside of your vocation.

☐ MY BOYFRIEND IS FUN . . .

Doesn't count. You need to establish an independent sense of fun. I have always dated men who took on the responsibility of being fun in the relationship. The problem with this is that one day you wake up (as I did) and ask yourself, "Do I love him or do I want to be with him because he's fun?" To preclude this scenario, and a terrifying sense of paralysis when you are left alone for a weekend, you need to develop your own ideas about what's fun, and take action all by yourself. (See "Fun Dates 101" later in this chapter.)

☐ I DON'T HAVE THE TIME OR THE MONEY TO HAVE FUN . . .

Yes, you do. You don't have to go away for a retreat in Sedona. Go horseback riding one afternoon, camp out with a girlfriend overnight, or peruse a flea market. There are countless cost-effective ways to have fun.

Big Fun List

Come up with ten specific things you would enjoy doing if money and time were no object—and, yes, you may use ideas from the jealousy list above. Then jot down a contact name and number, because above all things the list should be practical—those numbers should be there waiting for you when you're finally ready to take the plunge. If you like, you can break the list down into categories, such as big fun, quickies, sports, luxuriating, etc.

1. Fun idea: _____

    Contact: _____

2. Fun idea: _____

    Contact: _____

3. Fun idea: _____

    Contact: _____

4. Fun idea: _____

    Contact: _____

5. Fun idea: _____

    Contact: _____

6. Fun idea: _____

    Contact: _____

7. Fun idea: _____

    Contact: _____

8. Fun idea: _____

    Contact: _____

9. Fun idea: _____

    Contact: _____

10. Fun idea: _____

    Contact: _____

Once a month, I force myself to schedule something from my Big Fun list. For example, I've always wanted to go on a Disney cruise. Forget my son. I want to go. Lucky for me, my son wants to go, too, so I've made reservations for a trip this very summer.

Circle one fun thing you will do this month AND call the contact to arrange it.

Fun Dates 101

To build my muscle for independent fun, I've developed something I call the Fun Date. Though distinct from Big Fun, the Fun Date will also help rejuvenate your overly serious soul. These outings tend to take only an hour or two and are intended to be done alone. I recommend keeping a list of possible Fun Dates in your journal so you can decide to do one on a whim.

Go on a Fun Date once a week. You could: visit a museum, take a bike ride, enroll in a pottery class, go to the movies, or walk to a fair or the local pier. Do some brainstorming; you'll be surprised at the things you come up with on your own.

> "The man who has no imagination has no wings."
>
> —MUHAMMAD ALI

Make a list of ten Fun Dates you can do nearby your home:

1. _____

2. _____

3. _____

4. _____

5. _____

6. _____

7. _____

8. _____

9. _____

10. _____

Pick one Fun Date from the your list and do it this week. (For best results, go on a Fun Date every week for the rest of your life.)

This Week's Lesson

Having fun is a healthy way to blow off steam and stimulate yourself as you work toward your goals. There's a reason "all work and no play makes Jane a dull girl" is a cliché—if you ignore your need for fun, you will stagnate. I don't care how hard you're working in the rest of your life. On the other hand, the more fun you have, the happier you'll be and the easier your transformation will become. You'll reach your goals in no time—after all, who hasn't lost track of time when she was having fun?

Swan Secret: Find time for fun and pretty soon you'll find fun in everything you do—and your transformation will occur a lot quicker.

Sex

Does Sex Bring You Pleasure or Panic?

One afternoon, when I was little, I was standing in the kitchen with my mother while she made dinner. I handed her the onion she requested, and then I said, "A kid in school told me that when you grow up you put a boy's penis in your mouth."

My mother did not spit out the piece of apple she was eating. She didn't say, "Oh that's disgusting," or attempt to wash my mouth out with soap. In fact, she looked me dead in the eye and smiled.

"Don't worry about it," she said, "someday you'll like it." She went back to her cooking, and I went back to school with the knowledge that sex was not only normal, but also something to look forward to.

Now, I realize how lucky I was to have been raised by Hispanic parents who cherished sex and sensuality as an important, joyful, necessary part of life. From my vantage point, sex seemed as essential to an adult's existence as a job or a car. As a Latina, I was taught to hold out for sex and to value my virginity. But once I found the right guy, I was encouraged to have a really good time. In fact, it never occurred to me that someone might view sex as shameful or embarrassing until I began discussing the subject with non-Latinas.

Again and again, women I knew described sex in what to me were alien terms; many considered it a tedious and annoying chore. A tragic number identified it as one of the most problematic areas of their lives. Either they didn't enjoy it and became irritated when their husbands or boyfriends asked for it, or they wanted it more than the men in their lives. For the Swans especially, sex was a painful issue.

As a Swan you must *own* your sexuality. You must get in touch with *pleasure,* because physical joy is as essential to your growth as breathing. Owning your sexuality isn't about having a perfect body or physical prowess. It isn't even about love when it comes down to it. *Women need sensual pleasure.* Period. We need to be touched and caressed. We need to be cuddled. Without it we cannot be confident and vibrant; we cannot become the women we want to be.

If Sensuality Were Happiness . . .

If a baby of any species isn't touched and caressed, it will die. It doesn't matter if a human child has all the food and toys she could ever need; she cannot live without the pleasure of human contact. Though, as adults, we can technically survive without it, our need for touch does not diminish as we grow older. Being touched makes our blood flow better, our skin brighter, and our senses more alive.

Accessing your sensuality doesn't necessarily mean having sex. It could mean a shoulder massage or a foot rub. It could be someone tickling you. It could be a luxurious facial. Sensual pleasure of any kind will help you feel your body, nerve by nerve, heightening your arousal and your sense of peace and relaxation.

> "It is impossible to live pleasurably without living wisely, well, and justly, and impossible to live wisely, well and justly without living pleasurably."
>
> —EPICURUS

Pleasure Principle

How much time each week do you allow for sensual pleasures? An estimate is
fine: _____

What sensual activities give you the feeling of being truly inside your body? List
your favorites (whether you enjoy them regularly or not).

1. _____

2. _____

3. _____

4. _____

5. _____

Being Provocative in Bed

Does Sex Bring You Pleasure or Panic?

1. Does the thought of coming home from work only to find your boyfriend or
   husband *in the mood* bring you panic? Yes ☐ No ☐

2. Do you ever have sex just to *get it over with?* Yes ☐ No ☐

3. Do you ever fake your pleasure? Yes ☐ No ☐

If you answered yes to any of these questions, you need to be more proactive in
your sex life.

As with everything you do in life, if you're not getting something out of your sex life you're
going to start getting resentful. Waiting for things to happen to you may be very female, but it
isn't going to make sex fun. You've got to take action to get what you want. You must create
your ideal sex life.

I reminded one Swan of this recently, and she looked down at her feet, embarrassed. "I'm not sure *what* I want."

Sex is a sensual pleasure, like a massage or a hot bath. Think of it as a quick, if intensive, full-body spa vacation. In other words, consider the sensual pleasures you enjoy outside of bed to understand what might also work in bed. Review your list of sensual favorites, above, if you need to.

The Swan in question admitted that sometimes she visits the local nail salon for a foot rub. "A half-hour foot rub really relaxes me," she said. "It makes my skin come alive."

A foot rub may be the key to arousal for this Swan. Now she has to go about getting it. To this end, I offered some controversial advice: "Demand that your boyfriend rub your feet for a half-hour before sex."

Well, this Swan looked at me as if I were speaking Chinese. "That won't go over very well," she said. "A half-hour's a long time."

No, it isn't. I'm not saying you should make your request like a drill sergeant. Do it as a woman who is craving your lover's touch. Say with a combination of naughtiness and sweetness: *Oh my God, when you rub my toes it makes me . . .* You get the picture. Ask for what you want, even if you have to be a little "girly" about it.

---

1. What do you get out of sex? Be honest. An orgasm? A feeling of closeness? A rush of energy?_____

    Explain: _____

    _____

    _____

    _____

2. What sensual pleasures might help you get to where you want to be?
    a. _____
    b. _____
    c. _____

3. Ask for one of these pleasures *tonight.*

Sex and Your Mind

Now that you've identified what you need before sex, let's focus on determining what you need during sex.

Though men and women tend to think of intercourse as a very physical act, it's actually an activity of the mind. At least for women. That's why, for example, the anticipation before you have sex with a partner makes the actual act so *hot*. You've imagined it hundreds of times; you've fantasized about it. Those thoughts, as you may recall, make your nerves stand on end. They make you sensitive to every touch, kiss, and slap. Fantasy is a fabulous tool of arousal. Maybe it hasn't been working for you because you haven't made an effort to figure it out . . .

I realize, of course, that the idea of fantasy can be terrifying. Some people tell me they fear their fantasies are too weird, or they're worried that they might find themselves compelled to act on the kinkiest of them, which is extremely scary. That's not the way fantasies work. If you fantasize about sleeping with a woman, it doesn't mean you have to do it, and it doesn't mean you are a lesbian. You're simply letting your mind visit a place that makes you feel sensual. You are learning to let yourself go.

Now that we have that out of the way, let's access those dirty thoughts.

SEXY INSPIRATION

Sometimes it's difficult to conjure up a good fantasy. So why not steal someone else's? Movies and books are great for inspiring lusty imagery in our minds. What movie scene, for example, did you find so sexy that you wished you lived it? What book put you in the mood? Think of these books and movies as resources. Buy them. If you're too embarrassed to pick them up in a store, you can get them online.

Sex is like any other area in your life: It requires research. Feed your mind information and your body will respond.

> "For women the best aphrodisiacs are words; the G-spot is in the ears. He who looks for it below there is wasting his time."
>
> —ISABEL ALLENDE

BEDTIME STORIES

Another bedtime activity I find fabulous is talking in bed. Too few people capitalize on the steaminess of telling stories or talking their way through sex. Repeat a book's fantasies to your lover, or pull the book from the shelf and read it directly to him. For other occasions, make up a fantasy of your own. Talk to him about the different things you'd like to do to him (again, you don't have to actually do it). Then, ask him to reciprocate. You may surprise each other.

Sexy Bedtime Books

The Secret Garden, Nancy Friday
Story of O, Pauline Reage
Sleeping Beauty Novels, A. N. Roquelaure
Delta of Venus, Anaïs Nin
Vox, Nicholson Baker

Buy an erotic book and read a hot paragraph or two to your boyfriend or lover. *Tonight.*

This Week's Lesson

There are many ways to *own* your sexuality, and all of them should be fun. Pump yourself with information and share it with your partner. Demand—sweetly—those things that give you pleasure, because sex will enhance your confidence . . . and your ability to achieve your loftiest goals.

Swan Secret: Become confident in the bedroom and you will exude strength outside of it.

Community

What Have You Gotten This Month Without Asking For It?

I ask this question of the Swans when they arrive in Los Angeles. Usually, they reply, "Nothing."

Really? So, you didn't get a sample in the mail, a call from an old friend, a little extra whipped cream on your mocha? I jog their brains.

"Well, when you put it like that . . ." Suddenly they remember. It's that simple. A little shift in perspective and anyone can acknowledge the sweet moments in her day, no matter what else is happening. *Community* is about learning to appreciate those moments and the people behind them, about being mindful of all those happy details we too often overlook, and doing your best to reciprocate.

We spend so much of our lives complaining about the things that go wrong, but we never stop to ask ourselves what we've done to make things right in the world, not just for us, but for other people. That's why, on the first Monday of every month, I take a few minutes to give myself the third-degree: *Have I helped an old lady cross the street? Did I give a few dollars to a worthy cause? When was the last time I spoke to my grumpy cousin, the bane of the entire family?* In short, have I gone out of my way for anyone recently?

In his inaugural address in 1961, John F. Kennedy implored the country: "Ask not what your country can do for you, but what you can do for your country." Similarly, discovering your sense of community requires that you see yourself in the context of the energy you are sharing with the world. After all, if you're not putting anything out there, can you really expect to get anything back?

Grumpy or Giving?

What did you do or give this month without expecting anything in return?

1. _____

2. _____

3. _____

4. _____

5. _____

Create Your Own Good Mood

I spent a lot of time with a depressed Swan who could not see her way out of her own narrative of grievance. She often complained that nothing in life ever turned out right for her and that other people were making her miserable.

So I asked her, "Can you tell me what makes you so pleasant to be around?"

She looked back at me with a great deal of surprise. "What do you mean?" she demanded. "I have as much right to be happy as anyone else."

"Sure you do," I agreed. "But they have a right to expect you to be agreeable and pleasant."

This Swan was missing the point. Contributing wasn't going to be a larger burden on her soul. On the contrary, it would instantly lift her mood.

As the mother of a little kid, I have some experience with mood-altering tactics. On the rare occasion that my son throws a hysterical tantrum, for example, I'll point out the window and say, "Hey, what's that?" The next thing I know he's happy as a clam, examining the truck on the road beside us. Doing this to your child is known as *pattern interruption therapy*, and it works for adults, too.

As grown-ups, we wake up and think, *I'm in a bad mood*, then spend our day wallowing in the marsh of our own minds, oblivious to all the good things around us. The thing is, if you're looking to get out of your funk, you might start by opening your eyes. Say someone at the office is wearing a pretty dress, and you actually notice it. "Gee, Bonnie, that looks really good on you."

The fact is, it's almost impossible to remain despondent when you're busy complimenting someone, when you're busy spreading good cheer. Putting positive energy into the world is a real miracle cure. It'll get you out of that black hole of self-absorption in no time flat.

PUT SOME POSITIVE ENERGY INTO THE WORLD

You have the power to change your mood. You have the power to change the way you respond to the world and the people around you. And it's really not that hard. A little self-directed attitude adjustment makes everything easier to manage. Suddenly the world becomes full of possibility and you feel wildly optimistic.

Now take some of that positive energy and share it with the people around you.

Within the first hour of leaving your home (today or tomorrow), give of yourself without expecting anything in return. It could be a compliment, a smile, a thoughtful little gift. Situations will present themselves throughout the day, and all you have to do is act on them.

1. As soon as you can, report back to identify your *act of community* as well as the effect it had on your mood.

   a. Act: _____

   b. Effect on mood:_____

APPRECIATE THE MOMENT

The lovely thing about getting out of your own space and taking the time to compliment someone is that it makes you live in the moment. If you tell a colleague that she looks great in her dress, for example, you'll suddenly find that you are outside yourself. You are no longer obsessively reliving that

> "What is a cynic? A man who knows the price of everything, and the value of nothing."
>
> —OSCAR WILDE

traumatic phone conversation you had with your boyfriend last night, for the thousandth time. Instead, you are sharing a moment with a suddenly very happy colleague, changing both her day and yours. And look how little effort it took!

The moments of our lives are fleeting. Whether or not we acknowledge them, they appear for an instant and never return. Recognizing them by putting forth positive energy is the only way we have of being grateful. In the same way, many people in our lives are here for a short time. People move on, switch jobs, and disappear from our lives. We must learn to put some effort into showing how much we appreciate having them in our lives.

List every person you are grateful to have in your life right now:

1. _____

2. _____

3. _____

4. _____

5. _____

6. _____

7. _____

8. _____

9. _____

10. _____

List every person you are grateful to *have had* in your life for a while:

1. _____
2. _____
3. _____
4. _____
5. _____
6. _____
7. _____
8. _____
9. _____
10. _____

List every *thing* you are grateful for in your life:

1. _____
2. _____
3. _____
4. _____
5. _____
6. _____
7. _____
8. _____
9. _____
10. _____

You have a lot to be grateful about, don't you?

This Week's Lesson

Offer your energy to others, and you will find yourself living in a place of gratitude that will help you appreciate *all* the moments of your life, and you will get to where you want to be a lot more swiftly.

Swan Secret: A compliment a day keeps the doctor away.

> "Hold every moment sacred. Give each clarity and meaning, each the weight of thine awareness, each its true and due fulfillment."
>
> —THOMAS MANN

Health and Fitness

How Many Hours a Week Do You Spend on Yourself?

Putting the Pieces Together

While the television Swans were still working with our doctors, trainers, and dieticians, they were already mapping out plans for their post-show *swanning*—the beauty, fitness, and health routines that would help them maintain their new selves and reach future goals. It's true that they had already made big changes and that every single one of them was going home beautiful. But without a daily practice to maintain these improvements and to inspire new ones, all of their efforts would go to waste. You see, as Swans, our work is never done. Doing it gets easier. Committing to exercise and self-reflection becomes less of a struggle. But no matter what we accomplish, we forever remain works in progress. Being a Swan is a state of mind; it is a beginning, not an end. Our new selves require nurture, labor, and enduring passion.

What Is Your Current Health and Fitness Routine?

To establish a routine for yourself, you need to come to terms with where you are *now*. Take a moment to estimate the amount of time you spend on yourself.

1. How many hours a week do you spend on fitness? _____

2. How much time each year do you spend on your health? (visits to the doctor, dentist, gynecologist, the organic market, health club, etc.) _____

Constructing Your Routine

We're not born with routines. I never saw my mother spending money to take care of herself. She didn't get facials with any regularity. In fact, she never put herself first; she said our family couldn't afford it.

As with all the other skills I've developed along the way, I've established my routines by imitating people. I looked at who I was jealous of and what they were doing to maintain themselves physically. My first boss at *Seventeen,* for example, took care of herself in a way I didn't know was even allowed: she was always getting highlights, manicures, and going to the gym. I liked her results and I copied them.

Later, I encountered a lot of models who took great care of themselves. Of course, their position was "It's my job to be beautiful," while everyone around them didn't take care of themselves. When I started working in television, I realized that all the stars of the television shows took care of themselves but the people behind the scenes let themselves go. I thought, *Why is it that only the people in front of the camera take care of themselves? Why do they think they're worth more?* I decided then that I was going to act like one of them. I'm worth that no matter what my job title. We admire stars because it seems as if they have something we can't have. We tell ourselves it's their *job* to be beautiful while ours is taking care of our kids or sitting behind a desk. The truth is that we've imposed these restrictions on ourselves.

When it comes to my routine, I act like a star. So should you.

Name a celebrity muse who takes great care of herself: _____

It is time to take a closer look at your reflection. Where are you on the path to becoming a Swan? What issues do you still need to address? What areas of your life need maintenance? What will comprise your routine?

A word of caution: Some of your routine will cost money, and *all* of it will take time. At some point you're going to find yourself worrying about this and becoming discouraged. Well, you can't do that. You are your own best investment. Start treating yourself properly.

DOCTOR'S APPOINTMENTS

I schedule all of my doctor's appointments in January *for the whole year.* Do you go to the doctor on a regular basis? Make your appointments today. (Check the box when you've scheduled a meeting.)

_____

☐ Gynecologist—an exam is recommended once a year.

      Last visit: _____

      Next visit: _____

☐ General MD—a checkup is recommended once a year.

      Last visit: _____

      Next visit: _____

☐ Eye Doctor—an exam is recommended once a year.

      Last visit: _____

      Next visit: _____

      Services needed: _____

☐ Dentist—a cleaning is recommended once every six months.

      Last visit: _____

      Next visit: _____

      Services needed: _____

☐ Dermatologist—a checkup is recommended once a year.

        Last visit: _____

        Next visit: _____

        Services needed: _____

_____

Fitness

The Swan trainer advocates working out *at least* three times a week for an hour, minimum. Four times a week is better, and five times a week is even better than that, but start slow and work your way up. And remember, if you're not sweating, you're not working hard enough. (And this is about you, so *work*.)

FITNESS SUGGESTIONS

Walking is a good place to start. Running is even better. There's also weight-training, yoga, and Pilates—all of which are wonderful. At some point, consider working with a personal trainer, even if you can only afford him once every few weeks.

_____

1. Consider the kind of exercise routine your muse would follow:

    a. Days of the week she would work out: _____

    b. Exercises she would do: _____

    c. Duration of exercise per session: _____

> "Think like a queen. A queen is not afraid to fail. Failure is yet another stepping stone to success."
>
> —OPRAH WINFREY

2. What can you commit to every week this month?

    a. Days of week you will work out: _____

    b. Exercises: _____

    c. Duration:_____

3. Sign on the dotted line.

    I promise to adhere to my fitness routine all month.

    _____
    Signature

Nutrition

Almost every woman I know has trouble in this area. It is the area that I most consistently fall off the wagon—but then I get right back up and eat my spinach. There's help available everywhere.

    Television Swans go to diet counselors. There are similar options available to you (Jenny Craig, Weight Watchers, etc.), as well as online diet centers, and countless books covering every imaginable diet on the planet. Take a little time to do the research. Find a routine that works for you.

1. Describe your muse's perfect diet: _____
_____

2. In a few sentences, describe your current routine:_____
_____
_____

3. Now describe the way you intend to change your routine:_____
_____
_____

"Someday is not a day of the week."

—UNKNOWN

"I believe life is constantly testing us for our level of commitment, and life's greatest rewards are reserved for those who demonstrate a never-ending commitment to act until they achieve. This level of resolve can move mountains, but it must be constant and consistent. As simplistic as this may sound, it is still the common denominator separating those who live their dreams from those who live in regret."

—TONY ROBBINS

4. Sign on the dotted line.

I promise to adhere to my nutrition routine all month.

_____
Signature

Having the proper routine is the final touch—as well as the most important—on the new you. You can't be an ugly duckling if you follow a daily regimen toward self-improvement. These habits are your building blocks and your stability; they will help you make steady progress toward your goals no matter what happens in your life. They will bring together everything you've learned so that you can confidently present yourself to the world as the woman you want to be.

You're going to fall off the wagon occasionally. That's life. I eat junk food sometimes even though I know I shouldn't. It doesn't mean I'm throwing in the towel. I just get right back in there and keep trying.

This Week's Lesson

Spending time and money on yourself is not selfish, it's self-preservation. You will only walk this earth once; you deserve to do it exactly as the woman you want to be. Following a routine will put that bounce in your step and keep you moving forward every day of your life.

Swan Secret: Don't skip your routine on the bad days—it's the thing that will keep you balanced.

Beauty

What Do You Do to Maintain Your Appearance?

Let's be honest, feeling good about ourselves has a great deal to do with what we look like. In fact, the two usually go together; happy people radiate beauty and unhappy people radiate unhappiness. Now that you've worked so hard to transform your interior, it's time to let it shine!

Beauty is a major component of Swanning. Whether you are a model or not, putting effort into your appearance and feeling good about the image you project gives you confidence, and, perhaps even more importantly, it gives the rest of the world the cue to treat you with the utmost respect. Like everything else in *The Swan Curriculum,* beauty is about daily maintenance—waiting too long to get a wax or to get your hair done may not be a big deal to the rest of the world, but it will leave you feeling subpar, and affect your whole attitude. In this chapter you will take some time to determine what makes you feel pretty, confident, and comfortable in your skin—so you can look as good on the outside as you're beginning to feel on the inside.

> "Beauty is the gift of God."
>
> —ARISTOTLE

Beauty Is in the Eyes of Your Beholders

Are you doing everything you can to project the image you want to the world? Do you feel great when you have a manicure but your nails are always chipped? Do you wish you were ten pounds slimmer? Whatever is bothering you, write it down.

Constructing Your Routine

Beauty is not everything, but it is your most visible quality. Whether we like it or not, people treat the polished, well-dressed woman with the radiant smile a lot differently than the overweight lady in stained sweats and a mustache fit for a man. Why not do as your muse does and invest in your appearance? It's easy and fun, and you'll find it boosts your mood as much as any chocolate bar.

Pretty Woman, What Do You Do?

What does your muse do to feel pretty? Spend some time brainstorming to come up with as many hair and beauty rituals as you can.

1. _____
2. _____
3. _____
4. _____
5. _____
6. _____
7. _____
8. _____
9. _____
10. _____

Circle all of the above services you believe would accentuate your beauty.

Now that you've established what you need to feel great about your appearance, you must commit to a daily routine so that you can get there. For example, if you enjoy being a blonde but you're really a brunette, you've got to go in to the colorist every six weeks—don't wait for the roots to show! If you feel confident when your skin is clear, you need to go to the facialist every month. Your routine is the key to maintaining your new image as a Swan, but more importantly, it will help you keep an even keel. No matter what happens in your life, if you are following your routine, you will be able to keep it in perspective.

Take some time to consider the different areas of your appearance that could either use some work or require regular maintenance. Then devise a schedule for action all your own.

SKIN

You don't need to overdo the makeup if you're taking good care of your skin. If you get regular facials, and you pluck your eyebrows with care, you'll be amazed at the change. Looking good isn't about looking like a doll. Good skin projects a healthy glow, and you shouldn't cover up that glow with makeup. But you have to work at it; your skin, like the rest of you, requires regular maintenance.

I have a friend who refused to wear shorts for ten years because she had clusters of unattractive spider veins. Well, I told her to do something about it, and she did, and now I see her *only* in shorts. The moral of the story: Do something!

1. Identify the things your muse does toward maintaining healthy skin.

   At home: *Make-up? Tanner? Skin creams?* _____

   _____

   With the help of specialists: *Facials? Waxing? Endermology (non-surgical cellulite treatment)? Laser treatment for spider veins?* _____

   _____

2. What will you do every day as a part of your skin routine? _____

   _____

3. What services, if any, will you seek out through specialists? _____

   _____

HAIR

When does your hair look its prettiest? How often do you get a trim? Do you let a whole year pass with your hair pulled back in a messy bun because your split ends are so bad?

If you love those summer highlights, bring them back year-round! If your hair is getting shaggy, don't pull it back, go to the salon and get it cut. And don't skimp on the products that will make your hair feel soft and shiny—a deep conditioning can help you feel like a thousand bucks.

1. Identify the things your muse does toward maintaining healthy hair:

At home: *Deep conditioning?* _____

_____

In the salon: *Regular haircuts? Color?* _____

_____

2. What services do you need to seek out? _____

_____

Excuses . . .

I DON'T HAVE ENOUGH MONEY.
Yes you do. Services are available at every price range. If your weight is a problem, you can go to Weight Watchers (cheap!) or Overeaters Anonymous meetings every week (free!). For beauty services of all kinds, try a beauty school—they're so inexpensive my own mother's hooked!

I DON'T HAVE ENOUGH TIME.
There's always time. Yesterday I took my kid to karate and got a manicure and a pedicure while I waited. I simply squeeze it in. If I have to get up at six in the morning to get a facial, that's what I do.

BEAUTY IS SUPERFICIAL.
We have to get over this! We tend to think that people who take care of themselves are narcissistic. But, a CEO of a company is representing an entire brand. Should she really let herself go? Similarly, the mother of three kids has to visit school every day. Doesn't she want her kids to be proud of her? Shouldn't she strive to look great every day?

Very few people are drop-dead gorgeous. But you'd be surprised at how beautiful you can look, if you make the effort.

STYLE

I've heard Swans say, "I don't know what to wear so I don't go anywhere." Is this really a reason to be bummed out? As with everything else, developing a sense of style demands a routine. If you don't know how to dress, go hire somebody (see page 6). That's what I did!

1. How would my muse dress to go to the market? _____

2. How would my muse dress to go to work? _____

3. How would my muse dress to take her kids to school? _____

4. How would my muse dress to go out to dinner? _____

5. How would my muse dress to go to brunch? _____

6. What do I need to do to feel stylish (Hire a stylist? Ask a friend to take me shopping? Spend some time researching boutiques?) _____

Plastic Surgery

All of the Swans underwent plastic surgery either to fix problem areas that had developed over the years (saggy breasts) or to alter unattractive features that had always bothered them. The Swan Cindy for example, was called "the witch" in grade school because of her pointy nose. All her life, the broken record in her head condemned her as ugly and she wanted to break it once and for all. The very first thing she talked to her surgeons about was her nose. And now? Cindy got her nose job and is a stunning—even bewitching—beauty.

Now, this does not mean you must undergo plastic surgery to be a Swan. On the contrary, if you are happy with your looks and feel that your body might be enhanced best with a strong workout regimen, then listen to yourself. On the other hand, if there is a feature on your face or body that bugs you, I say *change it.*

"One important key to success is self confidence. An important key to self confidence is preparation."

—ARTHUR ASHE

PHASE I

Would it make you feel better about yourself if you had those crow's feet removed? Do you want to get rid of the brown spots on your forehead? There are little things you can do to make yourself feel younger *without* actual surgery.

Do some research and make a plan for a consultation.

1. What facial rejuvenation does your muse undergo? *Botox? Laser surgery? Injections?*_____

_____

2. How often would she make self-maintenance appointments?_____

3. What services will you seek out this month to improve the look of your skin?

_____

_____

PHASE II

If you have decided that there are things you want to *change* about your body that cannot be done by diet and exercise alone, do some research on doctors in your area, and go in for a consultation.

There are three steps to finding a plastic surgeon:

1. Visit the American Society of Plastic Surgeons at www.plasticsurgery.org to find board-certified plastic surgeons in your area.

2. Visit the websites of the board-certified doctors you have found. If they do not have a website, request their "before" and "after" shots. Determine whose work you like best.

3. Narrow your choices down to three surgeons and call for a free consultation. See if you mesh with the doctor. Look at more before and after photos. Keep in mind that you should not necessarily have the same doctor do *all* parts of your body. These are specialists—find out what their specialties are.

1. Which cosmetic surgery services would your muse employ? *Face-lift or mini face-lift? Tummy tuck? Lip augmentation? Liposuction?*_____

   _____

2. Which services would you like to investigate?_____

   _____

3. Sign on the dotted line.

   I, _____ , promise to
   research doctors offering the kind of services I am seeking.

   I,_____ , promise to make an
   appointment for a consultation.

   _____
   Signature

Reward Your Hard Work

I give myself gifts to mark all the little and big accomplishments in my life—it's acknowledgment and added incentive. If it's a little thing, I'll give myself an extra facial or maybe a trip to an amusement park. If it's big, I get a big gift. When I became president of Telemundo, for example, I bought myself a watch I'd been admiring for years. When you reward yourself with a gift, it becomes a symbol of what you have accomplished. Why wait for someone else to recognize it?

Give yourself a present for accomplishing a task this month. Plan it out in advance. Whether it's going to yoga as scheduled all month or making all of your doctor's appointments for the year ahead, reward yourself with something extra you would have once considered extravagant.

Task: _____

Gift: _____

I don't deserve it...

When she first considered devising a routine for herself, the Swan Merline explained that she couldn't spend money on beauty because she had to buy her kids this and that and *"nothing is left for me . . ."* While we've been conditioned to believe that such selflessness is honorable, allow me to reiterate: *There is nothing honorable about treating yourself as if you are worth nothing.* Merline was doing more than depriving herself of facials. She was sending her kids the message that she deserved nothing and that they should treat her accordingly.

This Week's Lesson

Every Swan wants to be beautiful above all things. In fact, every woman I know wants to be beautiful—though she does not always admit it. Don't ignore your inner life, but find ways to make your exterior shine too!

Swan Secret: For an instant pick-me-up, do the one thing that makes you feel ultra-girly. (I run to the manicurist!) It'll give you the confidence you need to feel fabulous for the rest of your day.

Conclusion

Congratulations! You did it, Swan!

It's been twelve weeks of hard work, but you've done it! Even if you can't see all the results of your grand plan, you have mastered skills and tools to take you the rest of the way. If you have completed the exercises, you have learned what you want out of life as well as why you haven't gotten it in the past. But, most importantly, you've learned how to think about your life in a new way. You are now someone who sees possibility everywhere you turn. Change, after all, is about perspective, about striving, about never giving up or becoming inactive. Your life is manageable with the skills you've developed. Whenever you feel lost or overwhelmed, return to the book and work through the exercises that resonate with you. Remember, being a Swan is an ongoing process. I too, am a work in progress. I still go to therapy. I still read philosophy and self-help books. And, I go back to the Curriculum monthly to see where I am, to record my successes and to identify new areas that need work. I'm committed to growth because maintenance is the key to life. You must always strive to be better, stronger, and more beautiful, and to share your unique voice with the world. Use your work in *The Swan Curriculum* as a launching pad to propel yourself into the rest of your life.

Your new life is about to begin! But, before you go, here are a few Swan Super Secrets . . .

WOMEN NEED TO BE CHERISHED

Women spend too much time giving, giving, giving. We need to put ourselves in a position of receiving, where people give to us because we are worthy and deserving of love and assistance.

YOU ARE WORTH AS MUCH AS ANYONE ELSE

A woman who gets facials every month, who exercises regularly, and who works on her body and soul each day is treated differently by the world than the woman who shrugs and says, "I don't deserve anything."

If you want to be treated well in the world, you have to change. You have to respect yourself. You have to put some effort into becoming the woman you want to be. And in order to do this, you have to stay focused on one truth above all others: *I am worth it.*

TURN NEGATIVES INTO POSITIVES

Life is tough, yes. Bad things happen, and you can't always stop them. But you can certainly change the way you deal with these setbacks, large and small. It all boils down to perspective, to the way you look at things.

As I told the Swans toward the end of their tenure, the one thing I can promise is this: Life is going to throw some curveballs at you. Deal with it. Nine times out of ten, something good comes out of every situation, no matter how bad. Remembering this will help you manage the worst that happens to you.

YOU MUST HAVE FAITH

You need to believe you will be taken care of in this life. But you must also take action. There's an old saying: *God helps those who help themselves,* and I believe it. Faith and action are your secret formula. If you have both, you'll make it—and that's a promise.

Remember: Nothing takes you farther than taking one step in the right direction.

Good luck and God bless!

NELY GALÁN

"Traveler, there is no trail—you blaze the trail as you go."

—ANTONIO MACHADO,
SPANISH PHILOSOPHER

Notes